TEXAS RIVERS

TEXAS RIVERS

by John Graves

Photographs by Wyman Meinzer

TEXAS PARKS AND WILDLIFE PRESS, AUSTIN

First edition, 2002

Requests for permission to reproduce material from this work should be sent to
Permissions, University of Texas Press, Box 7819, Austin, Texas 78713-7819.

The paper used in this publication meets the minimum requirements
for American National Standard for Information Sciences—
Permanence for Paper for Printed Library Materials, ANSI Z39.48-1984.

Library of Congress Cataloging-in-Publication Data

Graves, John, 1920–
Texas rivers / by John Graves ; photographs by Wyman Meinzer. — 1st ed.
p.   cm.
Includes bibliographical references.
ISBN 1-885696-38-8 (hardcover : alk. paper)
1. Rivers — Texas.   2. Rivers — Texas — Pictorial works.   3. Texas — History, Local.
4. Texas — Description and travel.   5. Texas — Pictorial works.
I. Meinzer, Wyman.   II. Title.
F392.A17 G73   2002
976.4 — dc21
2002004965

Book design by Nancy McMillen
Nancy McMillen Design, Austin

Map illustrations by Jane Shasky

CONTENTS

A PREFATORY NOTE, WITH ACKNOWLEDGMENTS

This book is not a comprehensive or even a representative study of Texas rivers. Both Wyman Meinzer and I have special interest in the western parts of the state, and five of the six chapters here are concerned with streams on the sunset side of the 98th meridian, which Walter Prescott Webb considered to be the dividing line between eastern and western ways of life. Our one river to the east of that line — nearly as far east as you can get without leaving Texas — is the Neches, which we chose because we both liked it and also, I suppose, in order to show that we knew there actually were rivers and people in other parts of the state. . . .

The chapters, together with many of the photographs, were first published as a series of articles in *Texas Parks & Wildlife* magazine during a period of about three years. For use in the book, the sequence in which the articles appeared has been changed, and they have all been retitled and somewhat revised to make them fit together more meaningfully.

The main things that these rivers — some of them just sections of rivers — have in common is that they all flow within Texas, and that the country through which each one passes is typical of a distinctive part of the state. Those in the wide and varied region we call West Texas do share some historical memories from the eras of Indian warfare, northward trail drives, and so on, but the lands they drain, like the tone of their people's lives in the past and now, differ significantly, and in pictures and words we have tried to define some of those differences.

All the rivers too have suffered to some extent, often greatly, from modern mankind's manipulation and exploitation of their waters and their basins, and we have tried also to be honest about those matters.

Without the able help of a number of people, we would have had much skimpier knowledge to work with while producing the chapters and pictures in this book. It was heartening to find that every river and basin we chose to photograph and write about had its local enthusiasts, and that among these there was always at least one of scholarly bent who had delved deeply into the region's human and natural history and its lore. Some have written books that are listed in our bibliography. During much of my writing career I have been dependent on the insights of people like these, and I treasure them. They constitute one of the few remaining barriers against the deadly sameness that increasingly infests our world.

These friends willing to impart their knowledge and skills and perceptions to us are listed on the next three pages.

John Graves
2002

THE CANADIAN

Alvin Lynn of Amarillo. I suspect that what Alvin doesn't know about his native territory is not worth knowing. I'll never forget the look in his eyes when, on a helicopter trip up the Canadian valley, he directed us to where he thought the trail established by Randolph Marcy in 1849 might have passed, and there below us, cutting clear and white across rangeland, were the ancient parallel tracks of wagons headed for Santa Fe and the goldfields of California.

Others who helped us in the Canadian country were Jim Whittenburg IV, Jon Jarvis, Ed Benz, Bob Smith, and Tom, Mark, and Teel Bivins.

THE LOWER NECHES

James Smith and Aubrey Cole of the Neches — hunters, fishermen, and rememberers of the old East Texas ways. They received us warmly, filled our heads with fine talk, and filled our stomachs with catfish from their cherished river.

Helpers here also included Bill Magee, Jack McDonald, and Raymond Koso.

THE PECOS

Jack Skiles of Langtry and the Pecos canyon country, a good man to hit the thorny brush with. Rancher, educator, scholar, and archaeologist, Jack has the same kind of intimate wisdom about his home region that Alvin Lynn has about the Panhandle, and a store of delightful family tales about the past, some of which he has published. Above the canyonlands game warden Don Jackson, an intelligent and friendly man whom we met at the ruins of old Fort Lancaster, turned out to be a mine of information about his own environs.

Additional Pecos friends were Glen Ely, Patrick Dearen, Mike Cox, Lowell Woodward, Helen Carter, Gary Oden, Darrell Hargrove, Jason Wrinkle, Skeet Jones, and Ernest Woodward.

THE LLANO

Constance Whiston, skilled flyfisher and canoeist. She lives in Austin, but this river is a passion of hers which she was glad to share during a couple of beautiful floats and plenty of conversation. She also shared her familiarity with its literature.

Others who were kind to us along the Llano: Gus Kaderka, Tracy and Homer Martin, Bonnie Schmidt, Dennis Heap, and Bill Worrell.

THE BRAZOS CLEAR FORK

Members and descendants and in-laws of the Matthews family of Lambshead Ranch. During a period of more than forty years these bright people have been not only warm and hospitable friends to me and my family, but also sources of much information about their region. Also most helpful on the Clear Fork were Joe Barrington of Throckmorton, an accomplished iron sculptor and fine company on a river float, and A. V. Jones, who showed us some special places including old Fort Davis in Stephens County.

Other generous-spirited persons in this area were Barbara Ledbetter, Dale Riley, Mrs. Putnam, Carol Martin, Jim Alexander, Bob Snyder, and Larry Barton.

THE UPPER SABINAL

Greg Walton. I don't know how we would have done this one without Greg's presence and his immensely useful, freely imparted knowledge of his beloved Sabinal Canyon. His books of interviews with old-timers, which he started taping in the 1980s, are models of what such works ought to be.

Other friends in this lovely valley were Karen and David Camp of the Texas Stagecoach Inn, Billy Moore, Jim Mangum, Morris Killough, Clarence LeBaud, Gary Davis, Ronald Lee and Annette Long.

It is not possible to conclude this list without mentioning a friend who is not an expert on any of the rivers but without whom we would have had a greatly diminished topographical understanding of several of them. This is Wyman's old college buddy Knut Mjölhaus, a businessman and enthusiastic aviator, whose generosity with his time and his skill and his airplanes let us view these streams and their countrysides in a unique way.

The Canadian is a very significant

piece of river in scenic and human and Texan terms.

Its ruggedly beautiful valley, in places more

than forty miles wide from rim to rim, emphatically

separates the North and South High Plains . . .

THE CANADIAN

A Slash in the High Plains

Our main Texas Panhandle river, the Canadian, has a rather enigmatic name. The suggestion has been made that some anonymous early explorer thought it flowed into or out of Canada, but I have a hard time believing that anyone in that profession was ever so geographically befuddled. Another hypothesis is that the word is a corruption of the Spanish *cañada*, which means ravine or gully. If so, however, the Texas part of its valley, viewed from its rim or from an airplane, is one monstrous ravine indeed. Still another, the one that makes the most sense to me, is that early trapping and fur-trading French-Canadian voyageurs, wide wanderers in their heyday, canoed their way down the Mississippi, then up the Arkansas and into at least the lower part of this tributary, which therefore got named for them.

It is only in part a Texan river. In its 760-mile course from New Mexico's Sangre de Cristo range to where it joins the Arkansas in eastern Okla-

homa, the upper-middle segment that winds through our northern rectangle of counties is only about 190 miles long. Nor does this part always resemble what people think a river ought to look like. Except in periods of spate it tends to be a wide bed of sand and gravel with a thread of current down its middle, usually muddy from the "red-bed" strata over which it flows in places — early visitors' journals complain about emerging from a bath there dirtier than when they went in. And sometimes the river consists of just the sand and gravel, with the stream's main flow lurking underneath and only occasional pools to avouch its status as a waterway.

Yet it is a very significant piece of river in scenic and human and Texan terms. Its ruggedly beautiful valley, in places more than forty miles wide from rim to rim, emphatically separates the North and South High Plains — the latter being called usually the Llano Estacado. Elevated flatlands standing 500 to 800 feet above the

river's bed, the Plains are the remnants of a vast debris apron laid down by great rivers that gushed down from the Rockies millions of years ago, and the Canadian valley between them represents ages of erosion of that apron. Along the valley now, rolling scrub-sprinkled grasslands interspersed with layered cliffs and buttes, spire formations, gravels, stones, and boulder-jumbles constitute an open-air museum of the varied minerals and sediments deposited by those ancient floods.

Mainly ranchland and therefore less drastically altered from its original condition than areas where farming predominates, the Canadian country still has a healthy component of the flora and fauna that have always been there, with a few subtractions and additions. Cottonwood, soapberry, hackberry, juniper, and elm are the principal trees to be seen, along with mesquite, a relatively recent invader. Surviving wild inhabitants include white-tailed and mule deer, pronghorn antelope, mountain lions in limited numbers, bobcats, coyotes, foxes, beavers, along with any number of other creatures such as eagles and lesser raptors, small birds of many kinds, a diversity of rodents and reptiles, fish in the tributary creeks and especially in modern Lake Meredith toward the middle of the river's Panhandle run. There are even restocked elk on certain large ranches, and an occasional black bear. But the packs of gray wolves are gone, as are the wolves' (and earlier men's) preferred quarry, the Plains buffalo in their once-huge herds.

The valley's human past, much of it dimly perceived, has been extensive. In a rain-short region, the area has been a focus of people's activity for nine or ten thousand years or more, since the first ones showed up. Not only the river but also and especially its web of tributary creeks, flowing from springs of the bounteous Ogallala aquifer underneath the Plains and passing through little canyons protected from winter's blasts, have been havens for immigrants seeking shelter and sustenance. There have been a good many waves and kinds of such folk, and most left telltale traces in the form of artifacts, flint-chipping spots, campfire charcoal, kitchen middens, kill sites, petroglyphs and pictographs, or the remains of dwellings.

In Late Pleistocene times here, tough Paleo-Indian hunters and gatherers killed, among other quarry, now-extinct beasts like mammoth, giant bison, New World horses, and camels, using spears often tipped with the distinctively striped Alibates flint that occurs in deposits on either side of the Canadian at Lake Meredith. It is believed that, along with other people like them all over North America, they may well have contributed to the disappearance of these species. Their successors lived on the flesh of animals much like today's, plus the all-important buffalo and an assortment of wild greens, fruits, roots, and seeds. From about A. D. 1200 to 1500 a special folk, with cultural and trading links to the Pueblo tribes of what is now New Mexico, seem to have dominated the valley. Known to archaeologists as the "Antelope Creek Focus of the Panhandle Aspect," these hunters, potters, basketmakers, and planters of squash, beans, and corn lived in clusters of semi-dugouts, walled above ground with vertical slabs of stone, along the tributaries and the river. They not only shaped and used the Alibates flint themselves but dug pit quarries, still visible today, and traded the flint to outsiders covetous of its beauty, so that knapped Alibates projectile points and knives and scrapers have been found as far away as California and Minnesota.

This people stayed along the Canadian until Apachean tribesmen from the north, farmers and hunters too but not friendly ones, arrived in the area and presumably wiped them out or ran them off. The Apaches were here in 1541 when Coronado crossed the Canadian in his search for golden

Quivira — "Querechos," he called them. They were competent warriors, as later Spaniards found out, and were among the first Indians to learn to use horses. But beginning around 1700 their farming habits — which caused them to be in their *rancherías* during a couple of spells each year, planting and harvesting — made them vulnerable to a wave of even fiercer horsemen from the north, the migratory hunting people we know as Comanches. Within a short span of years the proud Apaches had been driven to fringes and rocky corners of their erstwhile domain, while the Comanche winners, with their allies the Kiowas, achieved control of the lower Great Plains from Kansas and Colorado to the Rio Grande, and routinely raided beyond the bounds of that empire.

By the late 1600s hunters from Spanish-ruled New Mexico had begun to make autumn horseback expeditions to the High Plains and their valleys in pursuit of buffalo, which they killed with arrows and lances for hides and jerky-dried winter meat. The knowledge these *ciboleros* gained of the country's wrinkles and crannies and trails and waterholes was utilized later by New Mexican traders, who came with their laden burros and cart-trains to the Canadian valley as well as to other valleys and canyons along the Caprock Escarpment which sharply defines the eastern edge of the High Plains. Somewhat protected at first by a treaty their governor had made with the Comanches in 1786, in the long run the traders were tolerated by the Indians because of the beads, iron tools and weapons and utensils, cloth, liquor, and other civilized delights they brought to exchange for hides, dried meat, horses, and whatever other items of value the Indians wanted to swap. Innocuous in the early days, this commerce later aroused rage in expanding Anglo Texas as the traders' goods began to include guns and ammunition and the barter-items proffered by the Indians increasingly came to consist of large numbers of horses, mules, and cattle taken in raids along the advancing

Anglo frontier far to the east and south, as well as other loot and sometimes captive white women and children. To frontiersmen the Comanches and Kiowas were prime and utter enemies (a view warmly reciprocated by the Indians themselves) and the term *comancheros*, as the traders were now called, became a Texas synonym for evil.

New Mexican sheepherders — *pastores* — came along in the wake of the traders, building patriarchal hamlets known as *plazas* in sheltered, well-watered places and apparently sharing the comancheros' easy relations with Indians. In fact, some of the pastores may have been part-time comancheros themselves. And a good many explorers visited the Canadian valley over the years, from early Spaniards and Frenchmen to nineteenth-century Anglo-Americans both civilian and military, with motives either commercial or scientific, or both. Major Stephen Long's expedition, seeking the sources of the Red River in 1820, came down the Canadian from New Mexico by mistake and made notes and maps. In the decades before the Civil War, the observant Santa Fe trader Josiah Gregg and Army topographers like James Abert, Randolph Marcy, Amiel Whipple, and others blazed trails through and across the valley and mapped its terrain. Their journals detailed the area's flora and fauna, weather, watering places, landmarks, local Indians, and other such matters. Highly useful to later travelers and tradesmen and soldiers, the accounts and maps were sometimes published back East and were popular.

Though the 1861–65 war disrupted Western military activity and gave the Comanches and Kiowas more opportunity than ever to raid and rob along the hated Texas frontier, after Appomattox the Army came back and tried to tempt or coerce them onto reservations in Indian Territory, now Oklahoma. This didn't work for long. Proud warrior-huntsmen resented the meager rations doled out to them in those places, and waxed furious over white hide-hunters' killing of the buffalo, the chief source of their food, clothing, bedding, lodges, and indeed their whole way of life. Hence in the summer of 1874 when about 700 warriors — Comanches and Kiowas with allied and equally angry Cheyennes and Arapahoes — assembled for revenge under the leadership of the half-white Comanche chief Quanah Parker, their first chosen point of assault was the camp of 28 buffalo hunters (and one woman) on a Canadian feeder creek in what is now Hutchinson County, where stood the earthen ruins of a short-lived adobe trading post and fort built in the early 1840s.

This Second Battle of Adobe Walls (a punitive Army foray under Kit Carson had more or less won the first one in 1864, but had found it advisable to leave in a hurry) is a stock bit of Texas history. Its details — the dawn attack by Quanah's host, their failure to use their numbers for tactical advantage, the sharpshooting hunters' dogged resistance that climaxed in Billy Dixon's fabulous and perhaps fabled deadly 1500-yard rifle shot, the ineffectual four- or five-day siege that finally petered out — are too familiar to need rehashing here.

This was one of several such clashes in Texas, Kansas, and Indian Territory, and retribution came swiftly when Generals Sherman and Sheridan sent five troop columns converging on the High Plains from different directions. The peak engagement of this "Red River War" was Colonel Ranald Mackenzie's victory in September of 1874 at Palo Duro Canyon, where his troops surprised a major encampment of Comanches and Kiowas and destroyed their horses, lodges, and winter supplies. Most of the not-happy campers managed to climb out of the canyon on foot, but the loss of their shelter and supplies and 1400 horses was a catastrophe that marked the end of their domination of the southern Great Plains. There were a few more forlorn fights here and there, but in June of 1875 when the last staunch holdouts, Quanah Parker and his band of 400-odd half-starved Quahadi Comanches, came to

Fort Sill and gave up, that was that.

Mackenzie's victory unleashed an epic binge of slaughter, the wholesale commercial harvest of the region's vast buffalo herds for their hides, because the hunters now had nothing to fear. The Texas frontier dissolved, and cattle ranchers, the outriders of American civilization, poured in with their herds. At first, before wells and windmills became common on the High Plains, these newcomers, like their primitive predecessors, preferred springfed country such as that in the canyons of the Caprock Escarpment, the rolling prairies just to its east, and the Canadian valley, where they ultimately displaced the New Mexican pastores from their plazas. Rustlers and other bad fellows flourished for a time; Billy the Kid, for one, showed up. Some of the new holdings were imperial, even after barbed wire did away with the open range and land ownership became the norm. The most famous of these, the XIT, contained three million acres including much of the Canadian's western drainage. Other big ranches abounded, and still abound today, for most of the valley is too rough for profitable farming.

As is true of all ranch country, the valley's communities are scattered and in general small. Most started out as ranch headquarters or railroad stops, and a number of such have disappeared, among them wild and woolly Old Tascosa near the river in Oldham County, which is now the site of the late Cal Farley's famous Boys Ranch. Others have shrunk, like Channing in Hartley County, once headquarters of the XIT and still a county seat. Still others subsist on ranch-oriented businesses and what comes their way from the valley's petroleum and gas fields, tapped since early in the twentieth century and still yielding enough to have made many oilmen and ranchers rich. A few valley towns were founded because of nearby oil discoveries, and of these the best-known is Borger

— itself so wild and woolly in the booming 1920s that the governor had to send in Rangers and troops to bring its bootleggers, prostitutes, con men, and murderers under some degree of control.

With the fast roads and easy communications of our time, though, the area's economy is linked less to its own towns than to busy Amarillo on the valley's southern rim, a hub of intersecting railroads and highways and a center for commerce, shipping, and industry. An important element in the city's business is its direct or indirect involvement with the immensely productive irrigated agriculture developed on millions of High Plains acres since World War II. Thereby hangs a tale with relevance to the Canadian valley. What it amounts to is that so much water has been pumped out of the underlying Ogalalla aquifer, to support this kind of farming, that the aquifer's level has dropped enough to make pumping costs uneconomic in some Plains areas and to dry up many of the springs that have dependably fed the Canadian's creeks since humans first showed up, making life possible there for its successive and varied kinds of people.

To complicate things further, the river's own flow has been weakened in our times, not only by the shrinkage of the creeks' contribution but also by the existence of three large reservoirs which divert water elsewhere and lose much through evaporation. Two of these are upstream in New Mexico, and the third is Lake Meredith near Borger, completed in 1965, whose water is used by a number of Panhandle towns and provides aquatic recreation for many people. Below its dam the old riverbed, once an expanse of sand and gravel kept bare by occasional sweeping spates and up to a mile wide in places, is now a brushy swath with an often dry narrow channel running through it — a change that has led to some interesting litigation. Under Texas law, a river's bed between its cut banks is usually in the public domain, and because that

wide strip of brush was so classified, it had become a haven for hunters, birdwatchers, and other outdoor types. But ranchers abutting those parts of the Canadian recently sued for ownership of the riverbed strip outside the narrow channel, on the basis that the original shores were no longer the stream's true cut banks. And they won their case.

Ranchers owning riverside property in the stretches above the lake tend to be envious of their downstream counterparts. Public land is scarce in Texas, and especially public land with few restrictions on its use, like the bare riverbed for many miles above Meredith. Especially on weekends, this strip near points of access can be aroar with the exhausts of four-wheelers, dirt bikes, and other motorized forms of assault on the valley's peace, and throughout the year it serves as a basis for trespass on the ranches by hunters, despoilers of archaeological sites, fence-cutters, and, I'm sure, many innocuous moseyers who just want a look at the harsh and beautiful countryside. It is hard to lump all such persons, even the dirt-bikers and ATVers, under Alexander Hamilton's haughty dictum ("Your public, sir, is a great beast!"), but it is hard too to blame the resentful ranchers, many of whom are responsible custodians of their land and all that is on it.

These ranchers have reason also to envy riverbank landowners still farther upstream. Texas water law is sometimes described as complex, and sometimes as a mess. The uppermost stretch of the Texas Canadian, from the New Mexico line to the vicinity of Boys Ranch, comes somehow under Old-Spanish law and belongs entirely to those persons whose lands adjoin it. . . .

The Canadian valley for me is not only a phenomenal series of landscapes sustaining creatures and plants that have always been there, but even more a repository of reminders of

LAKE MEREDITH'S WATER IS USED BY A NUMBER OF PANHANDLE TOWNS AND PROVIDES AQUATIC RECREATION FOR MANY PEOPLE.

its past, both natural and human. The blessedly passionate breeds of scientists known as geologists and archaeologists have found a wealth of such reminders and have sorted out many of their meanings, so that an observer in the company of such a person, or maybe just armed with a little of that knowledge, can find reminders in many places. Petrified redwood trunks, perhaps, from a time when an ancient sea's waves lapped on a nearby shore, a time long before the immense rivers laid down the debris that became the High Plains. Other manifestations of those earlier ages, like the lodes of handsome, maroon-streaked Alibates flint beside Lake Meredith, a metamorphosed dolomitic limestone that was shaped into tools and weapons by all the valley's Old Ones throughout the millennia . . .

Traces of the Old Ones themselves — chip-paved places where they knapped that flint into those tools and weapons; slab-house dugouts of the Antelope Creek Focus folk, now discernible only as sunken places surrounded by jumbled large flat stones; potsherds textured with cordmarks in the manner of that same people; the incised picture of a buffalo in a high sandstone niche . . .

Of the later folk too, closer to us in blood and time — things like still-visible double ruts across pastures here and there, carved by the wheels of comancheros' oxcarts, or by those of Anglo westerers' and soldiers' mule-drawn wagons as they bumped along trails mapped out by men like Marcy and Amiel;

a darkly corroded brass .50-caliber cartridge case; a shattered whiskey bottle; a barrel hoop; a rotted wagonwheel hub encircled by its rusty iron tire; a spur; a harness buckle . . .

Or the evocative almost-wholeness of a remote and deserted plaza hamlet built maybe a century and a half ago by New Mexican pastores in a little creek canyon, great cottonwoods along the still-flowing stream, mud-mortared sandstone walls, falling down in places, defining the corrals and the scatter of now-roofless dwellings. Standing on the canyon's rim and looking at these things not far below, hearing a redbird sing chew, chew, chew from a creekside bush, you somehow suddenly, sharply, envision a scene from the life that people lived here. Women chatting and joking in Spanish wash clothes at the creek; another smiles gently as she carries a clay jug of water toward a house whose cooking fire's smoke lazes upward against blue sky. Men talk in the corrals as they shear protesting sheep, dogs bark, a horse whinnies, children cry out at play beneath the cottonwoods . . . And you know it was a good life — isolated yes, tough in the Panhandle winters and during drouths and other troubles, but full of meaningful work and love and satisfaction.

You know too that there have been thousands on thousands of good, full, tough, meaningful lives led by the Canadian valley's differing waves of people, and that this matters to you. And that it matters without you, all by itself.

PETROGLYPHS ALONG THE
CANADIAN AND ITS
TRIBUTARIES ARE EVIDENCE
OF THE AREA'S LONG HISTORY
OF HUMAN OCCUPATION.

OPPOSITE: LANDRIGEN MESA IS PART OF THE
ANTELOPE CREEK COMPLEX, INHABITED BY HUNTERS
AND GATHERERS UNTIL ABOUT A.D. 1500.

PREVIOUS SPREAD: ERODED
BADLANDS LINE THE RIVER NEAR
THE TEXAS-NEW MEXICO BORDER.

THE DIN OF CLASHING LEAVES FILLS
THE AIR WHEN WIND SWEEPS THROUGH THIS
COTTONWOOD GALLERY ON THE RIVER.

SETTING SUN CASTS A GOLDEN GLOW
ACROSS LAKE MEREDITH, NEAR THE MIDDLE
OF THE RIVER'S PANHANDLE RUN.

NEXT SPREAD: WINTERS CAN
BE HARSH IN THE NORTHERN
PART OF THE PANHANDLE.

THE OLD TORREY RUINS, CIRCA 1874,
ARE AN EXAMPLE OF ONE OF THE *PLAZAS*
BUILT BY NEW MEXICAN *PASTORES*.

MESA HILLTOPS AND SAND SAGEBRUSH
BOTTOMLANDS DOMINATE THE
LANDSCAPE ALONG THE DRAINAGE
BASIN OF THE LOWER CANADIAN.

THE SHIMMERING HUES OF
GOLDEN COTTONWOODS SIGNIFY
THE ONSET OF AUTUMN.

FOG SHROUDS THE LOWER
CANADIAN'S MEANDERING
RIVER COURSE.

EARLY SUMMER BRINGS FRAGRANT HORSEMINT BLOOMS TO
THE LOWER CANADIAN. NATIVE AMERICANS MADE A MEDICINAL
BREW FROM THE DRIED LEAVES OF THE HORSEMINT.

Nearly all of the lower Neches River

traverses a wide, shallow, wooded valley whose natives'

ways and history have typified much of East Texas.

II

THE LOWER NECHES

A Piece of the South

In contrast, on the distant far-eastern side of Texas from the Canadian, the lower Neches river flows through a vastly different landscape. For those of us who live in the more open country of the central and western parts of the state, the wooded zone along our Louisiana border can be a little daunting. Blessed with copious rainfall, laced with perennially flowing creeks that feed strong rivers, shaded by forests except where they have been cleared, peopled with folk whose traditional attitudes, ways of living, and even manner of speaking hark back directly to the Deep South, the region at times seems foreign to persons accustomed to the drier prairies, plains, rocky hills, and the dialects of the rest of the state.

Yet not all that foreign. A lot of Texans, looking back a generation or two or three, can find that kind of country and that kind of people in their families' pasts. I myself have never visited East Texas, or even just passed through it, without a sense that, different or not,

it represents part of my heritage, for a couple of branches of my own forebears were out of the same Anglo-Celtic, forest-dwelling, pastoral and small-farming stock as those who began to settle this area in the early 1800s.

Most rivers are "people rivers," in that their waters and the attributes of their shores have helped to shape human beings from primitive times on down, forming the ways in which those human beings have lived and labored and regarded the world. Nearly all of the lower Neches River, a stretch of some 85 miles or so from Steinhagen Reservoir, where it is joined by the Angelina, down to the industrial and residential clutter beginning near Beaumont, traverses a wide, shallow, wooded valley whose natives' ways and history have typified much of East Texas.

Thousands of years ago, the region harbored tough meat-eaters who killed its abundant game with flint-tipped spears hurled with the throwing sticks

that archaeologists call by the Aztec-derived name, atlatls. Much later it was the domain of Caddos and coastal Atakapas — the former descended from the Mississippian Mound Builders and among the most advanced of pre-white Texans, and the latter among the most primitive. It was traversed by early Spanish explorers who apparently picked up the name Tejas, or Texas, from a word used by the Caddos to designate themselves, and named the Neches itself after a Caddoan tribal group.

Later still, Spanish missionaries and soldiers were sent east from San Antonio to thwart intrusions by the Louisiana French, establishing Nacogdoches and other less durable toeholds. But the valley's ultimate white settlers were American Southerners of a numerous yeoman class that has been much neglected by historians. Moving from Pennsylvania, Virginia, and the Carolinas south and west to newer states, generations of their people had evolved an independent way of life on the fringes of slave-based plantation society, sowing patches of food crops and running their livestock on the unfenced open ranges of the sandy "pine barrens" of the uplands and the rich, tangled bottomlands of rivers.

Some had a few slaves, but most had none. Their life was based on plenty of elbow room, and on cattle, hogs, subsistence agriculture, wild meat and fish and the techniques for taking them, along with an intricate traditional lore relating to use of the varied species of timber all around. Forests were the kind of country they had known forever, or what passed as forever among Anglos on this continent. Here in the shaggy valley of the Neches, where the original Indians had been decimated by European diseases from Spanish times onward, such folk found plenty of land into which they fitted without having to change their ways.

It was a hardworking and chancy life, but in early days a full and satisfying one as described in the reminiscences of old-timers, the most interesting of which are those of a man named Solomon Wright, who grew up in the years just after the Civil War, before the area had begun to change radically. He wrote of prodigal numbers of deer and bear and turkeys and other game he had hunted, of cattle drives and cattle work in the thick timber, of hewing railroad ties, and of many other things he had seen and heard and taken part in. He had a lyrical appreciation of the world he had known there, and was capable of expressing it:

". . . In the spring of the year you could hardly hear your ears for the birds hollering and singing. It hardly seems like real living to me to be where you can't hear hoot owls, whip-poor-wills, and mockingbirds."

A bright scientist I once knew in Washington, a Geological Survey hydrologist, agreed with my own somber feelings about past and present damage to the natural framework of our continent, but unlike me he had worked out a dispassionate view of it. The loss of our primeval forests and prairies, the extinction or increasing rarity of many species of living things, the disruption of our waters' flow and their pollution — all these evils and more, he believed, are the price we have paid for progress and prosperity and our nation's power, for getting to the point we have reached today.

Whether or not one sees that as a good bargain, the Neches and its valley paid a full share of the price. In the beginning the tall longleaf pines of its uplands — part of a belt of such timber stretching across the South from the Atlantic into Texas — grew up to four or five feet in diameter and could be as much as 400 years old, with an open grassy understory and occasional patches of treeless prairie. This species of pine was tolerant of frequent grass fires, whether natural or set by the Indians and white settlers to control vermin and underbrush and to bring on

new grass, and old accounts describe the uplands as being like parks, where wagons could pass with ease. Closer to the river a mixture of often huge trees of many species took over — oak, pecan, walnut, hickory, loblolly pine, magnolia, ash, basswood, holly, and the like, with willow and birch and gum and great cypresses along the banks of the Neches and its tributaries. The shaded, damp, brushy bottomlands, flooded and fertilized annually by big river rises in late winter and spring, were rich in nuts and fruits and switch cane. Deer and waterfowl and fish were abundant, as were even bison, arriving each year from farther west and grazing the tall grasses of the prairies, and there were plenty of predators like cougars, jaguars, bears, and red wolves. Back then, most of the lower Neches country was a part of what came to be known as the Big Thicket, some 3.5 million acres of dense woods interspersed with pine barrens and patches of prairie and stretching from the Sabine to the Trinity.

The area is much altered today. Change, slow at first, accelerated as time passed. Many years before any Anglos showed up, the Indians, content for long centuries with their plots of corn and beans and squash and all the wild meat and fish they could want, had fallen in love with European goods brought in for barter by the Spanish and especially by Louisiana French traders — firearms, iron tools, cloth, and trinkets. They paid for such treasures chiefly with deer and bear skins and the pelts of beaver and otter, of which thousands were brought in each year to white centers. In terms of the land's richness, this was still relatively light use, but heavier than had ever occurred there before.

When Anglos came they too felt the need of a few of civilization's blessings in the form of salt, coffee, flour, cloth, tools, weapons, and so on, brought in on wagons and pack-trains or, increasingly, on small paddlewheel steamers. The settlers tended to pay for these items in a way similar to that of the Indians, through exploitation of the land's resources. By

then the resources included not only wild things but crops like cotton, where it could be grown, and always open-range cattle and hogs, which not only provided fresh and cured meat and leather, but also brought good cash when driven in herds to the Texas coast or across the Sabine to Louisiana.

These people had been avid and expert stockmen for generations before arriving in Texas, though the thickly forested areas in which much of their work had to be done had shaped methods of handling cattle and swine that were quite a bit different from the cowboy techniques of the open country farther west. Lariats, for instance, were of limited use in dense woods. The primary tools here were skillfully wielded bullwhips and aggressive, well-trained dogs that could penetrate any tangle holding cows or hogs and could force them to go where their owners wanted them. The best of the dogs became legends and were cherished like family members.

Soon the value of the valley's trees in a thriving, expanding American economy became a dominant factor. The earliest settlers cut down minimal quantities of timber for private use as firewood, fence rails, building-logs and shingles and rived boards, and in order to clear patches of cropland. But before long big rafts of felled tree trunks began to cruise down the Neches to be sawed and milled in the new town of Beaumont, at first primarily species that grew in or near the bottoms and were relatively easy to move to the river as logs, sometimes being floated to it during the flood-rises of winter and spring. Cypress was esteemed for its durability, white oak for barrel staves, walnut for furniture and decorative paneling and trim, hickory for many uses.

In those early days, most of the big longleaf pines of the uplands were too far from the river to be skidded down through the tangled bottoms with oxen. But their long,

BY 1930, TIMBER OPERATIONS IN TEXAS, FROM SMALL TO HUGE IN SIZE, HAD LOGGED OFF EIGHTEEN MILLION ACRES OF PINE FOREST.

straight, strong trunks with resinous heartwood yielded premium lumber, and where they could be skidded, they were. This riverborne commerce swelled until after the Civil War, when Northern timber barons with deep pockets, having ravished the forests of New England and the upper Midwest, came south to buy up large tracts of timberland, or the logging rights on them, at bargain low prices.

Then railroads appeared, gradually replacing steamboats and log rafts, and the ravishment turned earnest indeed, all up and down East Texas. The stands of virgin longleaf were now accessible by way of the rail lines and their temporary spur tracks, called "tramways," which carried logging crews to the timber each day until an area was cut out, then were relaid in another virgin expanse. Major sawmills no longer needed to be near the mouths of rivers but were scattered around the woods as centers for company towns, with all the ills and abuses of such places. It is recorded that by 1930 timber operations in Texas, from small to huge in size, had logged off eighteen million acres of pine forest. Some companies of the "cut out and git out" variety harvested all the land they had access to and then decamped, leaving a social and ecological mess. Others remained and grew larger, moving in on the remaining bottomland cypress and other hardwoods and eventually, as the twentieth century advanced, replanting logged-off territory in tidy rows of quick-growing loblolly and slash pines. They are still the biggest employers in the valley, bigger than the oil companies whose predecessors created a few rowdy boom towns like Batson and Saratoga and Sour Lake in the early 1900s, while exploration and drilling were taking place.

Many Neches natives took part in both the devastation of the forests and the oilfield work, though few reaped much of the wealth these activities brought to others. Most clung

as best they could to their old way of life, diminishing now through change but still mainly based on a couple of cherished rights with only a shaky basis in common law. One of these was the right to run any number of cows and hogs on unfenced open range, regardless of who held title to the land. The other was the right to kill wild creatures wherever and whenever and however one wished, unhampered by game laws and seasons.

Wholesale logging had played much hell among these creatures from the time it became common, through massive destruction of habitats to which they had adapted over thousands of years. And the natives themselves, with their hogs and cows and their passion for hunting, had started to play hell not long after they arrived here, on a smaller scale but so steadily that some species soon began to dwindle. The first to feel heavy pressure were the predators that menaced the settlers' beasts. Cougars and jaguars were just about extirpated so early that the records are dim. Red wolves in shrinking numbers survived into the twentieth century, but ultimately extirpated themselves, so to speak, by interbreeding with coyotes that prospered in the altered countryside.

Black bears, which not only killed and ate hogs but were very edible themselves in winter when fat on acorns and other mast, were hunted down with packs of tough, courageous dogs, often the same ones that helped to handle their owners' half-wild livestock. So absorbing and exhilarating were these chases that accounts of special hounds and hunts and bear-fights have come down to us through the years, and a number of men got so enthralled with it that they quit farming and stockraising altogether and became, simply, bear hunters. The most famous of these was the legendary Ben Lilly, immortalized in J. Frank Dobie's writing, an Alabama native who hunted bears and cougars across the South's wilder sections, including the

Neches country on occasion, before such quarry grew scarce and he moved on to the Rockies to see what he could do with grizzlies. And this kind of avid hunting, along with the wrecking of the woods, took care of the Neches bears, very few of which have been sighted in many years.

As bears and panthers grew scarce, dog hunters turned increasingly to deer, which could be driven past shotgunners on stands and were harvested in all seasons. Dogs also were used to trail raccoon and fox and bobcat, while trappers were taking as many of these species as they could, along with mink, otter, and other furbearers. The loss of creatures less useful or harmful to human interests, like the ivory-billed woodpecker, occurred almost without being noticed except by a sprinkling of scientists. Carolina parakeets, beautiful crop-destroyers once common in the eastern U.S., were gunned down to extinction, and the fate of the passenger pigeons, which used to descend on the Neches valley in millions each winter, is one of our nation's sad stories. Thus the bounty of nature was draining away, and the resulting scarcity turned to destitution in the Great Depression of the 1930s, when many people who had left the region for jobs elsewhere, during World War I and the booming Twenties, came back home to live off the land, speeding up destruction. Deer and turkey and other edible wildlife nearly disappeared.

The old way of living was doomed by then. In essence, it had been doomed since the big logging began, but its own excesses, based on the ancient, innocent belief that the land's riches would last forever, had much to do with its ultimate demise, which commenced not long after World War Two. Towns grew larger, and townsmen not attuned to traditional ways did not especially enjoy seeing hogs and cows in their streets and gardens, or getting mutilated in collisions with them on the highways. Hence during the 1950s all the Neches counties voted in laws that required livestock to be confined behind fences on owned property.

On paper at least, these stock laws did away with the sacred open range and cut down on the natives' right to roam the woods at will. The laws encouraged timber companies and other large land-owners to fence their holdings and lease the grazing rights. Increasingly too, as the State of Texas began to restock the region with deer and turkey, such owners leased hunting rights to clubs made up mainly of city folks, and the state began to bear down on enforcement of game laws.

But the old-timers didn't give up that easily. From the time that enclosure began, the destruction of newly erected fences was common, as were "spite fires" in the new inflammable plantations of loblolly and slash pine. Some club and company structures were burned. Natives continued to run deer with hounds or to spotlight them at night in all seasons, and when law enforcers and landowners started shooting the treasured dogs, people started shooting people. These kinds of unpleasantness, though diminishing with time, went on until 1990, when the state flatly banned the hunting of deer with dogs and made the ban stick. The traditionalists had lost their fight; the underpinnings of a local way of life dating back over a century and a half had crumbled. Many of them, aging now, still resent that loss.

Even the river itself had changed. Upstream reservoirs now rationed its flow and reduced the annual, beneficial flood-rises of late winter and early spring. Most of the time these days it is a muddy, snag-infested, rather placid stream on which it is hard to imagine a steamboat or a log raft making any progress at all. The catfishing is good and the white sandbars fine for camping, but for pretty water you have to go to Neches tributaries like Village Creek or Pine Island Bayou.

Nobody in the past several generations has seen the Neches or its valley or its people in their prime. Nobody ever will again. This is true of all sorts of country in Texas and in

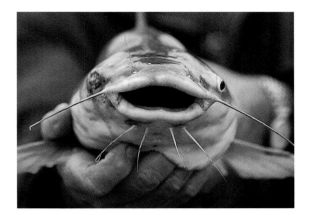

THE CATFISHING IS GOOD
AND THE WHITE SANDBARS
FINE FOR CAMPING.

most of the nation, and as a habitual backward-gazer, every time I'm reminded of it I feel a slight shock of anger. Not anger at anyone in particular, for what happened was what was going to happen. Just anger for not having experienced the rich and varied land as it used to be. I would have liked to thread through the fecund, often tangled Neches bottoms with their mighty hardwoods where thousands of birds sang and thousands of large and small animals roamed, and to have ridden among the upland groves of massive tall pines with their grassy understory. And would have liked also, I admit, to see the old steamboats chugging upstream, and to ride a log raft drifting down, and to sit by a fire under a sweet-gum tree and watch the faces of Neches men as their hounds' distant clarion voices told listening ears how closely they were trailing a bear or a panther. Because those were full-blooded parts of what used to be, and will not be again.

A *bit surprisingly perhaps,* enough of the natural framework of the valley is left, in scattered parcels, to give some sense of what the whole area was once like, and for that fact we are deeply indebted to people who for three-quarters of a century have been trying to obtain protection for as much as possible of what remains. Early defenders hoped to get up to 400,000 acres placed under Federal supervision, but later proponents — including the movement's modest patron saint, the late self-taught naturalist Lance Rosier of Saratoga — had to deal with political reality. The Big Thicket National Preserve, as authorized in 1974, consisted of 84,550 acres. In 1993, acquisition of another 10,766 was approved but has not yet taken place. The Preserve is divided into fifteen separate units chosen mainly in terms of how well they exhibit some of the ten distinct Big Thicket ecosystems, created by differences in elevation, proximity to water, and the qualities of soils.

Visitors, of whom there are many these days, can thus view tangled, soggy baygalls shaded by magnolias and hollies, or cypress sloughs where some of the old water-loving giants still stand, or huge hardwoods in the bottomlands of the river and its tributaries, or a number of other special kinds of woodland. They can canoe and fish the "corridor units" of the Neches itself and a couple of those tributaries, and can take part in trail walks led by knowledgeable Park Service rangers. Skilled birders with plenty of time on their hands can build up notable lifelists of the Thicket's resident and migrant avifauna, and in all of the units small mammals and reptiles and amphibians are numerous.

The only sizable animals still around are white-tailed deer, which are doing well, and the alligators that inhabit some of the Thicket's ponds and sloughs. As we have noted, bears and big cats and wolves have been gone for a long long time, and among the former Thicket habitats, the old patches of mixed-grass prairie are missing too, having been invaded by brush and loblolly pines in the absence of cleansing fire or, outside the Preserve, converted into fertilized tame pastures of exotic grass that produce quantities of beef per acre that astound and rather dismay cattlemen from farther west.

Tourism stimulated by the Preserve has brought a degree of prosperity to many local people, in the form of jobs associated with enterprises aimed at the alien influx — riding stables, canoe rentals, boat trips on the river, lodgings, guided tours, and the like. There are privately owned nature preserves, and two excellent state parks, one on Village Creek in the heart of the old Thicket and the other, Martin Dies, Jr., State Park, on Steinhagen Reservoir, which was Big Thicket too in its day. One tourist magnet, adjoining the Preserve on the north, is the small reservation of the Alabama-Coushatta Indians, peaceable people who arrived in the late 1700s and somehow managed to survive European diseases and other

AMONG THE FEW SIZABLE ANIMALS
STILL AROUND ARE THE ALLIGATORS
THAT INHABIT SOME OF THE
THICKET'S PONDS AND SLOUGHS.

dangers into modern times, while the valley's original Caddos and Atakapas died out or moved west.

And all over the map, on individual rural holdings or in small communities, live descendants of the old-time Anglo settlers, the legitimate heirs to a vanished way of life. In the boom times of the past half-century many of their young have moved away to prosper or perish in cities, and the ones who return are mostly changed, full of new ideas. But older natives still look back to the way things used to be. Some of these, having accepted change however ruefully, are hospitable to outsiders who like to hear their stories, of which they have many fine ones. I recently spent a couple of days among such people, running trotlines with a warm and competent man whose knowledge of the river's sandbars and snags and holes and bankside crannies was encyclopedic, and attending a fish fry where we sat up past midnight as good talk proliferated — talk of local characters and local feuds, and talk especially of hogs and cows and hunts with favorite dogs.

Other aging survivors still harbor a bitter resentment of change. They don't like park rangers and game wardens, and they want nothing at all to do with strangers.

And I, for one, can't blame them.

OPPOSITE: HUGE CYPRESS TREES, SOME
OF THEM HUNDREDS OF YEARS OLD,
GROW ALONG NECHES TRIBUTARIES.

LIGHT DIFFUSED BY
FOG HANGING ABOVE
THE RIVER BREAKS
THROUGH THE THICK
VEGETATION OF THE
NECHES AT SUNRISE.

OPPOSITE: BLOOMING FROM FEBRUARY TO JUNE,
VERBENA IS HEAVILY USED BY EARLY-EMERGING
OR OVERWINTERING BUTTERFLIES AND MOTHS.

{ PREVIOUS SPREAD: DROUTH
IS A COMMON VISITOR
TO THE BOTTOMLANDS.

POISON IVY ADDS AUTUMN COLOR TO THE
FORESTS SURROUNDING THE NECHES, BUT AVOID }
CONTACT WITH THIS THREE-LEAVED VINE.

COTTONWOODS AND CYPRESSES TAKE ON
HUES OF RED AND GOLD AS THE YEAR
DRAWS TO AN END ON THE LOWER NECHES.

NEXT SPREAD: DOGWOOD
BLOSSOMS SHIMMER
IN THE EVENING LIGHT
OF A PINE FOREST.

THE NECHES CUTS A MEANDERING
PATH THROUGH THE BIG THICKET
BELOW LAKE B.A. STEINHAGEN.

PINE TREES TOWER
ABOVE THE NECHES
DRAINAGE AREA.

STARK TREES REFLECT OFF
THE CALM WATER OF A
BLACKWATER SWAMP ON A
CLEAR WINTER DAY.

OPPOSITE: THE EARLIEST SETTLERS
CUT DOWN MINIMAL TIMBER FOR
FIREWOOD, RAILS AND SHINGLES.

The Texas part of the

Pecos River

is a mineral-laden

stream flowing for

some 350 contorted

southeastward

miles through

dry country that grows

harsher all the way.

III

THE PECOS

Tough Going

The Texas part of the Pecos River, from the New Mexico border to where it joins the Rio Grande, is a mineral-laden stream flowing for some 350 contorted southeastward miles through dry country that grows harsher all the way, much of it clad in spined desert scrub except where irrigation nurtures crops, though less abundantly than it used to. The region and the river have suffered a lot since their salad days, as has our whole continent. But this was hard country for people to live in even before whites showed up and began to exploit it.

The Pecos is generally regarded as the southwestern boundary of the Great Plains, whose swarming herds of buffalo stayed mainly east of the river, blocked not only by its treacherous currents, quicksands, steep banks, and heavy flow with huge occasional rises, but also by the usual scarcity of good water and dependable grazing on the other side. The latter-day horseback Plains Indians who subsisted on those herds stayed mainly to the north and

east of the Pecos also, except when riding to and from Mexico on bloody raids, along routes determined by the region's rare and treasured springs.

These days only infrequent big storms cause periods of heavy flow on the river, which has suffered the usual fate of Western streams in dry country — the interception of its waters, for irrigation and other uses, by big reservoirs upstream in New Mexico and at Red Bluff Lake just below the state border. Described variously by early travelers, according to where and when they struck the river, as anywhere from forty to a hundred feet wide and four to fifteen feet deep with a strong, fast, turbid current, the Pecos now only trickles much of the time and is more mineralized than ever. This shrinkage derives not only from the reservoirs but also from the enormous water consumption of the exotic saltcedars that infest its northern reaches, from Red Bluff past Mentone, the city of Pecos, and other towns whose names are familiar mainly to people in the oil business, places like Imperial, Girvin, and McCamey. The riverside lands in that section are generally level, though often with flat-topped heights in the background.

Below Sheffield, however, the Pecos enters deeply dissected limestone canyon country that continues all the way to its mouth on the Rio Grande at present Lake Amistad. This section has few roads and no real communities except for some along the railroad near the river's mouth, which have a colorful history involving outlaws and train-robbers and distinctive characters like Judge Roy Bean of Langtry. Most of the canyon area missed out on the West Texas oil boom, and its present inhabitants are chiefly sheep and goat ranchers who have developed ingenious methods of coping with perennial drouth, predators, and the rugged, thorny, sun-baked hostility of the terrain to human use.

Hostile though the canyon country may be, it is magnificent. The river in its high-walled gorge, though still much reduced in flow from its old self, is more like a river there. Strengthened and clarified and somewhat sweetened by spring-fed creeks coming in from some of the side canyons, it runs through pools and shallow rapids and boulder jumbles, talking as it goes. If you're willing to go to a bit of trouble to get there, it is a good place to be, with catfish and bass for sport and food, and hordes of birds in season.

Birds. . . . One April a few years back I canoed a stretch of that canyon part of the Pecos with some friends. It was not a luxurious trip for an outdoorsman with aging joints, like mine. The river was low, and to get through riffles we often had to wade, lurching over slick stones and dragging our boats toward deeper water below, which led to multiple aches at night but also to deep and satisfying sleep on gravel bars that were sometimes lumpy rock bars. We were wakened each dawn by bird calls and songs amplified by the gorge's walls —

canyon wrens and swallows that love high cliffs above water, falcons and hawks and eagles and ospreys and ravens, warblers and flycatchers and finches of many species, ducks, a wealth of long-legged, long-beaked shorebirds. . . . One morning we had a swarm of big handsome avocets — at least I think of them as a swarm though there were only twenty or so — that wheeped and flashed their black-and-white wings as they flew up and down the river for a time, wary of us, before alighting on a sandbar upstream. All these winged creatures, whether nesting or just passing through, were there because of the pull of a winding, rather puny thread of water in an intensely dry land.

This same thread of water, which used to be a lot less puny, has exerted its pull on many other creatures, including people. The earliest human prehistory of the whole Pecos region, insofar as it can be discerned, is not much different from that of other areas in Texas and New Mexico, dating back more than 12,000 years to a wetter and lusher time when ancient folk hunted now-extinct large creatures with spears, or ran them off of cliffs. A few thousand years later not only the quarry species but the climate had changed, becoming more desertlike, and people changed too in order to cope, or migrated elsewhere.

In the canyon country around 5500 B.C., a sparse population of stayers and copers had a primitive hardscrabble culture intimately attuned to their region's scant resources. Usually referred to as the Pecos People, they seem to have had no villages, for the land would not support concentrated use, as it still won't. Evidently they lived in small family or clan bands, migratory within a limited area, finding shelter in the canyons' overhang caves and devouring anything edible they could get their hands on, from bugs and reptiles and many kinds of plant food to fish and sometimes

red meat harvested with various weapons, the chief one being a flint-tipped cane dart or spear, given velocity by an atlatl. The bow and arrow, along with the Old World horse and other innovations, would not show up here until after these people had left the region or been exterminated.

They lasted for a long time without changing much — over 6000 years, till A.D. 800 or later — and they left clear traces of themselves. Making no pottery and erecting no dwellings beyond makeshift huts, they had an urge, whether esthetic or religious or both, to set down graphic proof of their presence in these rugged environs. That proof has come down to us most visibly on the walls of their cave shelters, in the form of great numbers of multicolored pictographs that have survived the attrition of time.

Some of these paintings are enigmatic swirls and shapes that resist interpretation, but others portray people and the creatures of that land. Predominant are bulky, often ornately robed figures with upraised arms that archaeologists call shamans, many of whom brandish the revered atlatl and spear. In some pictures droves of deer are scampering by, a few pierced by the shamans' shafts, and elsewhere warfare, or at least friction, is commemorated by spear-skewered prone human forms near a victorious shaman.

The thick floor-middens in the caves, representing millennia of accumulated debris and burials, protected by the overhangs and by the arid climate, add to what the paintings tell us about this people — their diet, their tools, their intricate use of local fibers for cordage and basketry, their clothing. . . . Some excavation of the middens has been haphazard and destructive, but much has been done with infinite care by trained persons. In one meticulously gathered and classified private collection that I visited in the region, a glass display case gave evidence that the Pecos People not only resembled us despite their style of life, but in some ways resembled us all too well. The case

held the skeletal remains of a woman and child; a projectile point was embedded in her hipbone and both of their skulls had been crushed by a club or stone.

A later people, possibly Apachean, also painted records in the caves, more literal in style and always in monochromatic dark red. And still others used black pigments here in historical times, with some of their work showing horses, cattle, and white people.

Early intruders of European stock were not enchanted by the beauties of the canyonlands. From the 1500s to the mid-1700s Spaniards probed at the region, Cabeza de Vaca on his long trek westward being possibly the first. After him various expeditions were all to some degree thwarted and confused by the maze of wide deep fissures spreading out through the lower Pecos country. In the end, having found no minerals there nor any Indians eager for Christianity, they gave up on the area. And as Apaches and Comanches acquired horses and deadly horseback fighting skills, the Spanish seem to have avoided the upper Texas Pecos too, sticking to their established settlements near the river's New Mexico headwaters and along the Rio Grande from the Sangre de Cristo range to the Gulf of Mexico.

A century after that abandonment, Anglos spurred by the territorial acquisitions stemming from Texas statehood and American victory in the Mexican War began their own probing of the area in search of military and commercial paths to El Paso, Santa Fe, and California. Their early expeditions came to the same conclusion as the Spaniards about the canyon country, and the ultimate main wagon and stagecoach roads and cattle trails ran north of that difficult patch. These routes soon got enough use, by Gold Rush emigrants and others, to attract Indian raiders, and in the 1850s a string of U.S. Army camps and forts was established along the usual roads west. The Texas posts were mostly abandoned during the Civil War and

Indians ruled the land again, but soon afterward when the Army came back and established a bit of order — not much of it for a good while — the flow of emigrants was augmented by Texas ranchers moving west and north with their herds.

Crossings — firm-bottomed places with sloping banks, fordable or swimmable by horses and cattle except in times of spate — were scarce on the Pecos with its steep shores, quicksands, mudbanks, and stretches of deep swift water. These few spots were sprinkled down the river from Pope's Crossing near the New Mexico line (under Red Bluff's waters now) to a little-used one at the mouth of Howard Draw in the canyonlands. What was known as the Lower Road, coming from San Antonio via Fort Clark and an Army post on the Devils River, forded the Pecos near Fort Lancaster just north of the canyons, going upriver from there and then cross-country to Fort Stockton. Before joining it, the Upper Road serving other eastern areas came toward the river through a notched ridge-pass called Castle Gap, then descended to the famous and infamous Horsehead Crossing, used by the Comanches on their old War Trail between the Panhandle and northern Mexico. It was named for the skeletons and skulls of horses and cattle that littered its banks, the victims of salty alkaline Pecos water, often in sun-concentrated overflow ponds above the banks, that they sucked up too eagerly after long dry drives. Charles Goodnight's heavy losses of cattle on his first drive in 1866 from the Brazos to Horsehead and beyond, when he and his partner Oliver Loving were feeling out the Goodnight-Loving Trail to upper New Mexico and Colorado, caused him to dub the Pecos "the graveyard of the cowman's hopes."

Although some wagon trains and traildrivers crossed at Horsehead, more including Goodnight and Loving watered their animals and themselves there (most old accounts of arriving thirsty at the Pecos complain bitterly about its taste), then traveled up the east bank to safer crossings. Safer at least in terms of cattle losses, though Comanches and Kiowas, in quest of loot and revenge on interlopers, harried the crossings and the trails, killing many drovers and emigrants and absconding with their livestock. On another drive in 1867 — the worst Indian year of all on the trails — Oliver Loving had a fight with such warriors up the Pecos and died later of his wounds, an incident that inspired Larry McMurtry's account of Gus McCrae's fate in *Lonesome Dove*.

The Indian threat lessened with the Comanches' defeat at Palo Duro in 1874, though Mescalero Apaches based in the Guadalupe Mountains continued to harass ranches and trail herds until subdued in 1881, and the country along the Rio Grande suffered Indian depredations out of Mexico, quelled in large part by the activities of a bold, tactically brilliant Army officer named John Bullis and his handful of Black Seminole scouts, three of whom earned the Congressional Medal of Honor.

Bridges at Lancaster Crossing had been built and had soon washed away in rises, but for stage lines and military wagon trains and those of freighters and emigrants many of the crossings had been superseded in 1870, when the Army built a chain-tethered pontoon bridge, rising and falling with the river's moods, beside Camp Melvin downriver from Horsehead.

In the early 1880s the completion of railroads — the Texas and Pacific in the north and the Southern Pacific across the canyonlands near the Rio Grande — further diminished use of the crossings except by local ranchers, some stubborn wagon emigrants, and traildrivers.

Despite Indian troubles, cattlemen had begun open-range ranching along the Texas Pecos in the 1870s, and when the troubles were past, except for a good many rustlers and other

outlaws, more ranchers started arriving with their herds. In the early days, when the Pecos was the chief source of water, ranching was generally restricted to a belt of country straddling the river and extending about twenty miles out on either side, the distance that hardy longhorn cattle could range and graze and still get back for a drink every day or so. Most ranchers used the land without owning it, and some of their operations were huge, preempting hundreds of thousands of acres. There was still a good bit of grass back then and overstocking was the rule, initiating range deterioration that would continue until recent times.

The cowboys who made such ranching possible shared the skills, routines, and sense of humor of other "hired men on horseback" then working the open range all the way to Canada, with a few altered methods and unique tasks imposed by the Pecos country. Their roundups, for instance, were more linear than those of the Great Plains, moving from camp to camp along the usable strips of land on either side of the river. And their job included duties unfamiliar elsewhere, such as "riding bog" to locate cattle mired in the river's quicksands, then extracting each by wading in and stamping alongside its legs to loosen the sand's grip, while a mounted partner on shore kept his lariat taut to the animal's horns, ready to pull.

In general, these cattlefolk were dry, hard, honorable people, but all was not harmony among them. Ranchers squabbled with ranchers over territory or cow ownership, and sometimes shot one another. Cowboys could be prickly too, especially in the heat and dust of drives, and many an unmarked grave lies lost along the old trails. Bad men were common in the earliest days, stealing cattle and horses, hijacking wagoners and emigrants, murdering, sometimes lording it over whole areas for a time until someone tougher and meaner showed up, maybe on the side of the law. Ironically, one of the best-known of all Western gunfighters, Clay Allison ("He never killed a man that did not need killing," claims his tombstone), ended up ranching very peacefully on the Pecos, running a couple of thousand cows at Pope's Crossing.

Most of our farming and ranching land has deteriorated since virgin times, but an arid stretch like the Pecos country, with around twelve inches or less of average annual rainfall, suffers much worse under hard use. The overstocking of the riverside strips in early open-range days was continued on a much wider scale in the 1880s when drilled wells with windmills expanded the usable grazing territory, and probably was made even more intense by the advent of barbed-wire fences, which let owners run all the cattle their acreage could hold, and then some.

The resulting damage to the land was compounded by natural disasters along the way. In the winter of 1884–85 a great blizzard drove many thousands of cattle southwestward from the Panhandle to drown in the Pecos, perish in its quicksands, or starve later, along with hordes of local cattle, on a drouth-stricken range eaten bare. That drouth lasted two years and at its height parts of the river were choked with carcasses, stinking to heaven. Such hammer blows, with variations, would strike again and again, each time driving many small ranchers out of business and some big ones too, while the land grew less and less productive. Just before another killer drouth in 1916–18, the carrying capacity of land in the Pecos country was said — with much optimism, I surmise — to be one cow on thirteen to eighteen acres. Today, according to a knowledgeable local man I visited with at old Fort Lancaster, that capacity is about a cow to 128 acres, if that, and the pastures hold far less grass than creosote brush,

cactus, catclaw, and scrub mesquite. Such country is better suited to weed-eating sheep and browsing goats than to cattle, and in most areas these smaller animals do now greatly outnumber traditional bovines.

More or less timely salvation for many surviving Pecos ranchers, and for other residents too, came in the classically Texan form of oil and gas. Most of the counties in the river's drainage are underlain by the famous Permian Basin, exploitation of whose riches began in the 1920s and has continued through the years, even though with ups and downs based on the Great Depression, a few wars, and the wavering price of oil.

Anyone familiar with oilfields and oil towns (and what Texan is not?) knows that they seldom generate scenic beauty, and parts of the upper-Pecos landscape are a cluttered mess to contemplate these days. But in the view of perhaps most people who inhabit that landscape, along with the mess have come money (often wealth), good jobs, vigorous new people, and a whole new way of existence. Whether that way is a true improvement on the old way of the hard-riding ranchers and cowboys is a nostalgic question that can be asked, but not very relevantly. In keeping with the practice of their times those old ones wore the country down remarkably fast, and had their day, and it was time for whatever came next.

Downstream, though, are still the Pecos canyonlands in their harsh magnificence, resisting change and civilized human use as they have always done. Lake Amistad has flooded the lowest sections and the river itself has been much diminished in flow, but the carved, rocky, dry, thorny, beautiful land is much as it was when the Pecos People scrabbled out a living there and painted their dreams, if dreams they were, on the walls of their caves.

PREVIOUS SPREAD: CASTLE GAP, THE RUGGED
GATEWAY TO THE PECOS, WAS A FAMILIAR
LANDMARK TO BOTH RANCHERS AND COMANCHES
IN THE MID-NINETEENTH CENTURY.

SOARING 300 FEET OVER THE
CANYON BELOW, A BRIDGE SPANS
THE RIVER NORTH OF DEL RIO.

WHITE CLIFFS RISE ABOVE THE
CONFLUENCE OF THE PECOS AND THE
RIO GRANDE IN VAL VERDE COUNTY.

CRYPTIC PETROGLYPHS ARE
A REMINDER THAT HUMANS
VISITED THIS REGION
THOUSANDS OF YEARS AGO.

OPPOSITE: PREHISTORIC
PEOPLE LEFT PICTOGRAPHS
IN ROCK SHELTERS
OF THE LOWER PECOS.

A GRAY FOX PEERS
THROUGH THICK DESERT
SCRUB NEAR THE RIVER.

MERELY A TRICKLE OVER MUCH OF ITS
COURSE, THE PECOS COMES TO LIFE IN
THE CANYONS OF THE LOWER END OF THE
RIVER AT PAINTED CANYON RAPIDS.

CAPT. JOHN POPE CAME TO THE PECOS
IN 1854 TO FIND THE BEST RAILROAD
ROUTE TO THE PACIFIC. THIS IS ALL THAT
REMAINS OF HIS LIVING QUARTERS.

NEXT SPREAD: RED BLUFF DAM AND
RESERVOIR, JUST SOUTH OF THE
TEXAS/NEW MEXICO STATE LINE,
INUNDATED POPE'S CROSSING IN 1936.

DOWNRIVER FROM THE CONFLUENCE OF THE PECOS
AND THE RIO GRANDE, AMISTAD RESERVOIR STRADDLES
THE BORDER BETWEEN TEXAS AND MEXICO.

HAND-SIZED PETROGLYPHS ARE
MYSTERIOUS REMINDERS OF
THE LONG-AGO HUMANS WHO
MADE THEIR HOME IN THIS
HARSH AND DESOLATE COUNTRY.

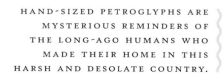

Born in limestone hills,

the Llano traverses a long

swatch of the anciently volcanic

Llano Uplift, a distinctive zone of

jumbled granite, metamorphic rocks,

upheaved sedimentary strata

and diverse minerals.

IV

THE LLANO

From Limestone to Granite

In Spanish a *llano* is a plain, a stretch of country like the high, wide, almost level Llano Estacado of the Panhandle. However, our river of that name, near the northern edge of the Hill Country, flows through no terrain of this description in its east-northeasterly course from sources west of Junction to where it joins the Colorado. In fact, much of the region it drains is decidedly rugged if often scenic, with canyons and mountains. Born in limestone hills, in its middle and lower reaches it traverses a long swatch of the anciently volcanic Llano Uplift, a distinctive zone of jumbled granite, metamorphic rocks, upheaved sedimentary strata, and diverse minerals of which some are unique to this area. About the most the river's uneven and brushy shores can muster in terms of flatness is an occasional floodplain of the sort the Spaniards called *vega*. So how came it to be called the Llano?

Linguists who ponder such anomalies have come up with an explanation

which an amateur has to suppose is accurate. It seems that the Native Americans inhabiting this region when the Spanish first explored it, in the early 1700s, were Tonkawan tribesmen called Chanas, or Chanes, so their main stream was dubbed the Río de los Chanes. Rather soon thereafter, these tribesmen left the scene as dire waves of first Apaches and then Comanches took over their landscape. Later Spaniards corrupted the river's name into Río de los Llanes or sometimes Llanos, "ch" and "ll" being fairly interchangeable in their language. Later still, nineteenth-century Anglo-Texan frontiersmen called it simply the Llano, and corrupted corruption by pronouncing the word "Lanno," as we still do today. Many Spanish place names in Texas, full of connotations, have been thus mutilated over the years, but sometimes they've gained other connotations in the process.

Because of hostile Indians, the Spanish never got a toehold on this stream. They built a fort and a mission

PREVIOUS SPREAD: EVEN THOUGH IT RUNS
THROUGH SOME STARK AND JUMBLED
COUNTRY, THE RIVER ITSELF IS A LOVELY
STREAM IN TIMES OF NORMAL FLOW.

NINETEENTH CENTURY SETTLERS
CONSTRUCTED HOMES FROM NATIVE
STONE THROUGHOUT THE HILL
COUNTRY AND THE LLANO BASIN.

on the San Saba, the next river to the north, but these soon suffered a disastrous assault by a large host of warriors and were abandoned in 1758. So stubborn was the natives' grip on the region that, although it was owned on paper by various grantees during Spanish and Mexican rule and into the period of the Republic of Texas, these worthies did not often risk their scalps by going there. Nor did other white men except a few hardy pokers-around, adventurers, and — especially — prospectors, among whom famous James Bowie was the most eminent and one of the earliest.

Bowie and others like him came because some nosy fellow had found a little smelter and a pile of silver-ore slag in the remains of the abandoned San Saba presidio, at the site of present Menard, and had spread the word. It was assumed that the ore had been dug up somewhere near the fort, and just about all the obsessed searching occurred in that neighborhood, not only in Bowie's time but for at least another century. Unfortunately all of these folks were looking in the wrong places for what came to be known as the Lost San Saba or Lost Bowie Mine. The Spanish really had had a silver mine, in a hill called Los Almagres for its red-ocher content. But it lay seventy or so miles southeast of their fort, in igneous Uplift mountains drained by the Llano, from whence they had brought the ore on burros to their base on the San Saba.

In the twentieth century a historian named Bolton, studying archives in Mexico, came across detailed documents concerning the mine, and afterward brought his scholarly knowledge to bear on the Riley Mountains south of the town of Llano, where he actually seems to have found the hill Almagres on Honey Creek. He and a friend undertook to extract its riches, but they came to the same conclusion that the Spaniards had reached long before, that the ore's silver content was too sparse to be worth the cost and effort of digging it out.

Some doubt has recently been voiced as to whether Bolton

found the right hill, nor has his experience been seen as definitive by treasure-hunters, a dogged breed. Some of them are still looking for the Lost Bowie Mine, or for stashes of its silver in spots where Spaniards pursued by Comanches buried it in haste. Or so most of the stories claim, more or less.

The river has two upper branches, the North and South Llanos, arising in Sutton and Edwards Counties respectively and coming together at Junction, the reason for that community's name. From there the main stem winds for about a hundred miles to the Colorado on upper Lake Lyndon B. Johnson, passing through a lot of rocky grazing land as it goes, and also through much backwater history.

The first white settlers along its banks, in the 1840s, were Germans out of Fredericksburg, people brought to the New World by the Society for the Protection of German Immigrants in Texas, called usually just the Society, or Verein. This impractical if philanthropic group of Teutonic noblemen, few of whom ever came across the ocean themselves, had bought sight unseen the settlement rights in a vast tract of land known as the Fisher-Miller Grant, stretching between the Llano and the Colorado. Then, before they went bankrupt in 1847, they shipped something over 7000 of their countrymen, mainly but not all peasant farming folk, to the port of Indianola on Matagorda Bay.

From there the immigrants were to be transported in wagon trains to the Grant, but there often weren't enough wagons or provisions, and the Grant turned out to be still dominated by Comanches. Therefore most of the newcomers were settled in and around way stations set up at New Braunfels and Fredericksburg, or died in epidemics, or dropped out in disgust and went elsewhere in Texas on their own. Some got to the southern edge of the Grant, along the Llano,

where the Verein before its collapse sponsored three settlements — Leiningen, Castell, and Bettina — of which only quiet, quaint Castell, on the river in western Llano County, has survived.

Bettina, not far from Castell, may be worth a glance. It was founded by a group of some forty university-educated free-thinkers seeking refuge from political turmoil in Germany. They envisioned a collectivistic paradise on the Llano, with shared labor on the land and shared intellectual idealism in the evenings in their large thatch-roofed common-house. They even made friends with a band of Comanches. But they got to quarreling over work loads, who were to be the bosses and who the peons, and other matters, and within a year all of them had given up hope and dispersed, though some did ultimately benefit Texas as doctors, engineers, scientists, and founders of solid families.

Soon Anglo-American settlers, primarily from the Upper South, were also flowing into the lower Llano country despite Comanches. From 1851 on, a protective Army garrison at Fort Mason attracted many of them, along with a continued influx of Germans, while downstream to the east the Anglo town of Llano was established in the middle 1850s. The Civil War and its aftermath brought dissension to this frontier, as they did to much of the rest of the Hill Country. Many of the German settlers, though not all, were against secession from the Union, while most Anglos sided with the Confederacy. Some violence resulted, as at the "Battle of the Nueces" in 1862, where an armed band of Unionist Germans on their way to Mexico were overtaken and decimated by a Rebel force.

Spilling over into the Reconstruction years, these antipathies manifested themselves most notably in the Mason County War of 1875–77, also known as the "Hoodoo War," one of that turbulent period's numerous local squabbles in Texas. Besides old ethnic tensions and lingering wartime passions, greed played a key role in the hostilities, for the cattle trails to

Kansas had recently turned nearly worthless livestock into property well worth owning, or stealing. A frequent casualness about whose calves were branded by whom, and whose steers were added to trail herds, led to bloody reprisals and counter-reprisals. Nor was there a shortage of drifting, lawless, deadly men rustling cattle on their own. To a large degree this strife ended up pitting "Dutchmen" against "Americans," and when the solidly Anglo Texas Rangers were called in to straighten things out, they did not always stay neutral. Some members of all factions perished or were maimed before the fighting petered out with the death, prosecution, or departure of its most violent participants.

Not long after all that, law and order and peace descended upon the region. Sheep and goat and cattle ranching, with some farming on patches of arable soil, were and still are the predominant occupations, though the prospect of riches from the Llano Uplift's varied minerals has sparked excitement from time to time. This kind of anticipation peaked in the 1880s and 1890s when it seemed certain that iron deposits in northwestern Llano County were going to be mined on a large scale. A boom began but petered out when nothing happened, and in the long run the most profitable mineral turned out to be the area's plentiful granite, valued for buildings (our State Capitol, for example), monuments, sculpture, gravestones, and the impregnable jetties that shield navigation channels on our coastline. All over the Uplift region this dense and durable stone crops out, most dramatically in the massive, bald, pink dome called Enchanted Rock, a Texas Parks and Wildlife State Natural Area now.

Up till now, most of the river has been spared from the fate of some other Hill Country streams — the preëmption of long segments of their shorelines by second-homers, retirement

THE RIVER HAS TWO OR THREE
LOW DAMS BUT NO LARGE RESERVOIRS,
AND IS CAPABLE OF GENERATING
DESTRUCTIVE FLOODS.

communities, and chichi resorts. It has two or three low dams but no large reservoirs, is capable of generating destructive floods, and a couple of times during the bad drouth of the 1950s, stopped running in its lower parts and exhibited its bare stone bed. Nor does the rough landscape it crosses in its course from the Edwards Plateau to Lake LBJ possess the green intimacy of, for instance, the cypress- and pecan-shaded banks of the Guadalupe and the Blanco. The few towns of its drainage basin, in general, lack the ethnic charm of Fredericksburg and Boerne and Comfort and other Germanic tourist meccas to the south. But probably the main cause of its preservation has been its relative remoteness from the megapopulations of Austin and San Antonio and the superhighway corridors that enmesh them, for most parts of it are not a short and casual commute from those places.

For however long things stay as they are — a quite dubious proposition in times like ours — the Llano remains one of a handful of decent Texas watercourses that have not been subjected to major hydrological alteration in the form of big dams, or significant development except at the retirement and recreation center of Kingsland, where the river becomes an arm of Lake LBJ, and at the upper end of things, near the thriving town of Junction, where lie some of the prettiest parts of the river's system, but where Interstate 10 from San Antonio has brought on something of a land boom. Much shoreline property there is now owned by absentee city dwellers and individual retirees, though so far without garish results.

Among the Llano valley's natives, of course, more than a few would like to see development thrive on any terms, for it is not hard to yearn for change if you dwell in tough country that doesn't often compensate hard work with wealth. Abundant cash these days resides mainly in the cities, and if by some means you can lure a bit of it to your own neighborhood, you may be able to share a few of the blessings of our enduring American prosperity. For a good many Llanoites, therefore, the anticipation of such an infusion of lucre may rival that which awaited a mineral boom in the late nineteenth century.

Traditionally, much of the urban cash that has found its way to the Llano country has been in the form of substantial lease money paid to ranchers by hunters, who pour in each year to harvest the area's abundant deer and turkey. Originally in response to this influx, and more lately to accommodate the growing numbers of non-sporting city people who have grown fond of the region and its communities, a considerable sprinkling of visitor amenities exists — restaurants, inns, bed-and-breakfasts, guest ranches, and the like, some of them old-style and simple and others quite fancy. The number of retirees is on the rise also. But most of these outlanders and new people, it seems, are there because they like things as they are. They are not a stimulus for big change.

The Llano's writers and artists also like what's there, though in some sections their increasing numbers and their different lifestyles are clashing a bit with local ways. (In Mason, for instance, I heard a grumpy native refer to his town as "Little Taos.") While some of these creative folk came here to live from distant parts of the country, most are from elsewhere in Texas. A few were born in the region, including sculptor Gene Zesch of Mason County, whose distinctive, warm-hearted, carved-wood caricatures of cowboys and other range characters are popular throughout the American West.

Then, too, there was the Llano country's main literary figure, the late Fred Gipson, who used his lifelong knowledge of this land and its people to shape best-selling works like *Hound Dog Man* and *Old Yeller*. Even after great success with his books and the movies made from them, Gipson retained his links to home terrain, living on a small ranch whose house's grounds dropped steeply down to his beloved Llano

River. We were friends, and I visited him occasionally there in the 1960s for perhaps a bit of fishing and certainly much good talk, for he was full of fine local tales of which only a few found their way into his writing. One that I recall concerned Herman Lehmann, a farm boy kidnapped by Indians, who became a full-fledged Apache and later Comanche warrior. Recaptured by whites and returned to Mason County, he had to relearn German and English and civilized ways, and became a local character. Fred remembered him as an old man who made annual appearances at the county fair, where he would show up on a horse in his Indian outfit, war-painted and armed with a bow and arrows. His performance consisted of running down a large calf released from a chute, killing it with his arrows, then dismounting and cutting out its liver, which he would eat raw while grinning bloodily at the horrified delight of the assembled onlookers.

Those were simpler times. . . .

Even though it runs through some stark and jumbled country, the river itself is a lovely stream in times of normal flow. Its purling clear water issues from good springs on its north and south branches, and is augmented by tributaries here and there, the main one being the James River, a scaled-down version of the Llano, on which I have met with a group of friends each April or May for the past twenty years or so. We camp and fish and talk for three or four days, cooking over a wood fire, wading upstream or down to cast our flies and lures into riffles and the blue-green pools below them. Our quarry includes big sunfish, small spotted and Guadalupe bass, sometimes sizable largemouths, and catfish taken at night on baited lines. It is not possible in that place to be unaware of the teeming wildlife dependent on the stream's crystalline flow. Birds in particular — both resident species and migrants, large and small, water birds and raptors and bright denizens of the thorny scrub of the hillsides — are strikingly apparent at that time of year in all their shapes and sizes and colors. The dawn chorus of their singing, though it can't be called harmonious, is the finest alarm clock that has ever called me out of slumber.

Almost any place along the main Llano is like that too, and usually has more water and more fish. A good many segments of it are navigable in a canoe or kayak, though other long stretches are so intricately strewn with boulders or gravel bars that shoving and pulling your craft through to relatively open water can take up more time than paddling. Much of the river also — for instance, most of the eighteen or nineteen lowest river miles from the town of Llano to above Kingsland — is not only tough boating but also tough to reach, for there are few access points and private ranches line its banks. This is a bit hard on recreationists but probably good for the river itself, since those sections get lighter human use and play a considerable part in maintaining the stream's overall health, including fish populations.

One of the most pleasant and feasible Llano floats is another stretch of eighteen or so miles along the river's south branch running north-northeast to Junction, through limestone country well upstream from the Uplift zone. Points of access are plentiful at road crossings, private pay campgrounds, canoe-rental places, and the South Llano River State Park, so you can choose whether to undertake a strenuous trip or a short and easy one. Freshened and replenished not far above by the famous Seven Hundred Springs that issue from a low limestone bluff — an age-old Indian site on a ranch that used to belong to Texas Governor Coke Stevenson — the river winds clear and cool through long pools separated from one another by narrow, willow-draped rapids.

It is not a wilderness stream for, as observed above, much

of the shoreline in that area has been broken into the small holdings of vacationers and retired people. Especially on weekdays, however, as you glide along the steep-banked river, you observe few signs of human activity beyond an occasional stairway down to a landing or a swimming platform. On a recent springtime float, a friend and I saw no people at all, but did see deer, wild turkeys, great blue herons, vul- tures, ducks, innumerable small birds, and a barely glimpsed aquatic furbearer — beaver, nutria, otter? — that swiftly hid itself amid some overhanging bushes. The season was early for good fishing, but on light fly rods we caught and turned loose enough feisty Guadalupe bass and sunfish to justify the outing in anglers' terms.

In terms of pure pleasure it amply justified itself.

SPRINGTIME BLUEBONNETS GROW
THICK ALONGSIDE THE JAMES
RIVER, THE LLANO'S MAIN
TRIBUTARY AND A SCALED-DOWN
VERSION OF THE LLANO ITSELF.

BLACK-TAILED JACKRABBITS
AND WHITE-TAILED DEER ARE
AMONG THE WILDLIFE THAT
THRIVE IN THE LLANO BASIN.

RARE PERIODS OF EXCESSIVE RAINFALL
RESULT IN DANGEROUS FLOOD CONDITIONS
ALONG THE FLOOD PLAIN OF THE LLANO.

PREVIOUS SPREAD: SUNRISE BRINGS
PINK AND GOLD HUES TO A FOGGY
PECAN GROVE ON THE LLANO.

SHALLOW POOLS OFFER MIRROR
IMAGES OF AQUATIC VEGETATION
ON THE NORTH LLANO.

PRAIRIE CONEFLOWERS CREATE
A PALETTE OF COLOR
THROUGHOUT THE HILL COUNTRY.

NEXT SPREAD: THE LLANO CUTS
A MEANDERING PATH THROUGH
A FOG-SHROUDED LANDSCAPE.

THE RISING SUN PEEKS OVER THE GENTLY FLOWING
LLANO, ONE OF ONLY A HANDFUL OF TEXAS
WATERCOURSES THAT HAVE NOT BEEN SUBJECTED
TO MAJOR HYDROLOGICAL ALTERATION.

A FULL MOON HANGS OVER THE LLANO,
ORIGINALLY EXPLORED BY THE SPANISH IN
THE EARLY 1700S AND SPARSELY SETTLED —
FOR THE MOST PART — TO THIS DAY.

GRANITE FROM THE LLANO UPLIFT REGION
HAS PROVIDED BUILDING MATERIAL
FOR STRUCTURES ACROSS TEXAS, INCLUDING
THE STATE CAPITOL IN AUSTIN.

Among the rivers and river-branches
that traverse the Rolling Plains, it would
be hard to find one more typical than the
Clear Fork of the Brazos.

THE BRAZOS CLEAR FORK

Cow Country

Most Texans with any interest in such things agree that the basic methods of ranching and cowboying in the American West were shaped up in our state, growing out of long-established Mexican ways of handling half-wild livestock on unfenced ranges — lariats, horned saddles, roundups, branding irons, and all the rest. These practices prevailed in the 1700s and early 1800s in the country from San Antonio south, and on the western Louisiana prairies and nearby parts of Texas, regions where cattle-raising with a strongly Hispanic flavor was the principal use of land.

The pattern was somewhat modified by cowmen coming in from the older Southern states, but remained for the most part intact. Perhaps its most typical form, as disseminated up the expanse of the Great Plains during a dynamic period of thirty or forty years, was to be found in the grassy, subhumid Rolling Plains of near West Texas, an area drained by the Colorado, Brazos, and Red rivers and extending from

approximately the West Cross Timbers to the canyoned fringe of the Llano Estacado. This section was settled predominantly by Anglos. Its early ranching history coincided with the final decades of the Comanches' and Kiowas' fierce resistance to white encroachment, the extermination of the buffalo herds, the great trail drives of longhorned cattle to Colorado and Kansas and beyond, the establishment of fabled ranches all the way into Canada, and barbed wire's ultimate triumph over the open range. All that was of course the classic West as commemorated — sometimes well, though more often falsely — in a multitude of books, movies, and TV serials, and it lives on in the minds of people all over the world.

Among the rivers and river-branches that traverse the Rolling Plains, it would be hard to find one more typical than the Clear Fork of the Brazos. This is a usually placid stream that burbles from one long tree-lined pool to another, winding some 140 generally north-

eastward miles from sources near Snyder, passing through prairie valleys and part of the Cross Timbers before joining the main-stem Brazos in Young County. Because so much of the river is bordered by undeveloped, sparsely peopled land and there are no high dams along its course, you can easily imagine, while paddling down it between dirt bluffs in the shade of willows, cottonwoods, pecans, and elms, that you are seeing the Clear Fork as it has always been, as it was in virgin times.

Imagination, however, can be a tricky thing. This river, like nearly all of our rivers, is much altered from what it was like in the old days. Back then abundant prairie grasses — sustenance for roaming hordes of buffalo and antelope and mustangs — had laid down spongy topsoil that absorbed rainfall and rationed it out to streams, producing steady flows in all but the worst drouth years. But the prevalent overgrazing of the open-range period (and often later, for that matter) bared that topsoil and let much of it wash off in stormwaters or blow away on the West Texas winds. In consequence, waterways like the Clear Fork became more "flashy," flooding their shores during wet spells and shrinking when the country was dry. In addition, a massive invasion of mesquite, low brush, and prickly pear on the abused land drank up much of the available moisture.

In modern times, the river's hydraulics have been further affected by the presence, on tributary creeks, of a couple of sizable reservoirs that draw off much water for use by towns and local industries, and by an upstream "scalping station," where pumps squirt additional quantities through a pipeline toward the faucets and lawns and swimming pools of prosperous Abilene. With dubious generosity, this city returns a part of the water to the Clear Fork in the form of sewage effluent, improved somewhat in recent years by updated treatment plants but still not much appreciated by riverside people for many miles downstream where, during periods of low flow, mounds of detergent foam form at narrow places, the stream's aroma can be less than idyllic, and its fish are generally limited to hardy species like carp and catfish.

No, not virgin. But it is still a pretty and peaceful river most of the time and in most reaches. And it is richly endowed with history.

As in just about all other parts of the continent, ancient hunters roamed the basin of the Clear Fork thousands of years ago, when it was far different in climate, vegetation, and native animal species. But those people left no record of themselves beyond occasional artifacts and kill sites. By the time Spanish explorers began to encounter and list the natives of the region, the predominant tribesmen were Apaches. In their turn, as noted earlier, these farmer-hunters were displaced by the nomadic Comanches, whose reign in most of our Rolling Plains lasted for the better part of a century and a half. Along the Clear Fork their menace held the Anglo frontier pretty much at a standstill for about twenty years.

Ranchers and farmers started coming into the eastern part of the Clear Fork country in the middle 1850s, encouraged by the presence of federal troops at such spots as Fort Belknap on the main Brazos, Fort Phantom Hill north of present Abilene, and the garrisons at two Indian reservations. The troops also furnished protection to westbound wagon trains and to the stagecoaches of the Butterfield Mail that started rattling through on journeys to and from California in 1858.

Camp Cooper was the post at the Comanche reservation straddling the Clear Fork in Throckmorton County. Some of its officers would be famous a few years later — Robert E. Lee, Albert Sidney Johnston, George H. Thomas "the Rock of Chickamauga". . . . The reserve held some 450 Penatekas or southern Comanches under a chief named Ketumse, and for a time

at least they seemed willing to think about farming as a way of life, even though their first unskilled attempts at raising crops were blighted by a bad drouth.

The other, larger reservation was on the main Brazos near the mouth of the Clear Fork. Its nearly 40,000 acres were populated by about 2000 less warlike Indians displaced from their old homelands by the whites' inexorable advance—Caddos, Anadarkos, Tonkawas, Delawares, Wacos, Choctaws, and the like. Most of these tribes had an agricultural background and soon were working the land so productively that the reservation's future seemed bright.

For a while, at any rate, it seemed that way. Some of the region's white settlers were tolerant of the reservation Indians and made friends among them. Others, though, despised all red men whether bellicose or peaceful. Tracing back to the frontiers of Virginia, the Carolinas, Tennessee, and the cotton states, this hostility was kept alive now by zealots who blamed the reservation Indians for all livestock losses and incidents of petty thievery, and even for the Penatekas' untamed cousins' continuing forays. Various hostile acts by the Indian-haters climaxed in a confrontation at the large Brazos reservation, a battle nearby between Indians and whites, and a sad decision by the Indians' supervisors to move all of their charges, including the Penatekas, to Indian Territory north of the Red River, which was done in 1859. The reservations were again unoccupied land, part of the open range.

During the next year and a half or so, before the Civil War erupted, settlers kept arriving in the Clear Fork country, the Butterfield continued to roll through, Comanches raided for horses, loot, and scalps, and Army units and Texas Rangers pursued them across the prairies, with occasional successes that kept them wary.

The war changed this pattern most unpleasantly for white residents. With the federal posts abandoned or taken over by small bodies of state troops, and a good many young settlers off fighting for the Confederacy, the vengeful red warriors' incursions grew more frequent and bloody. Stagecoaches stopped running, and many whites moved back east to more thickly settled areas. Those who stayed often "forted up" with other families in makeshift compounds here and there.

One of the most moving places I have seen along the Clear Fork is a small hillside cemetery above a riverbottom flat where one such compound stood. Called Fort Davis after the Confederacy's president (there was no connection with the Army's old Fort Davis far out toward El Paso), it was a two-acre quadrangle of impermanent picket cabins containing some stubborn families, about a hundred persons in all, who were tired of fighting off Indians on their own and alarmed by an especially gory raid involving hundreds of warriors in the fall of 1864, along Elm Creek not far to the north.

The fort served its purpose, for there were no direct attacks on it, though some conflict occurred between the Indians and settlers who went out on patrol or for the purposes of hunting meat or tending livestock. It had a school, and there were even festivities on occasion. In the morning after one party, moccasin tracks showed that silent Indians had come near and danced to the fiddle music for a while, before untying some visitors' horses and riding them away.

But life there was hard, with supplies from outside nearly impossible to obtain, and rudimentary shelter, clothing, and medical care. Just how hard is shown by the graves in the little cemetery under its shady live oaks — thirty in all, according to records, of which seventeen with lichened stone markers are still visible. Most settlers left the fort to return to their own ranches within a year or so after the war finally ended, and all seem to have departed well before the Army came back in 1867 and, on a height above the Clear Fork in Shackelford County, established Fort Griffin. So many deaths in a popula-

tion of a hundred, within so short a time, constitute a notable mortality rate. . . .

Fort Griffin quickly became one of the most important frontier posts, from which troops — often black "buffalo soldiers" freed from slavery by the war — rode forth to do battle with the wild raiders, when they could find them. In these sallies they were aided by scouts from a band of Tonkawas encamped east of the fort, survivors of a massacre of their tribe in Oklahoma by other Indians.

Settlers resumed their herding and farming, and the trail-driving to northern cattle markets began from all ranching parts of Texas. Soon the fort's presence on its hill led to growth of a town on the river floodplain below, a bawdy, brawling, and nearly anarchic community known as "the Flat," where legitimate merchants and traders operated cheek by jowl with a floating assortment of prostitutes, gamblers, con artists, sometime lawmen like Wyatt Earp, Doc Holiday, and Pat Garrett, outlaws like John Wesley Hardin, and many other fringe frontier types, all there to make money off of the soldiers and off of one another.

Activity in the Flat became still livelier after the autumn of 1874, when Mackenzie's victory over the Comanches and Kiowas in Palo Duro Canyon not only brought cattlemen and farmers swarming through to take up new land, but also turned the buffalo-hunters loose. Griffin town became a main market for thousands on thousands of stacked, dried, stinking hides, a supply point for the hunters, and a place for them to blow their cash on whiskey, women, and cards — or to lose it, sometimes along with their lives, to the town's abundant criminals. It was still the Flat, but some now called it Hidetown, and by 1875 it was also a source of supplies and entertainment for the drovers of cattle herds moving up the Western Trail.

This was the era of Reconstruction, that bitter time when Civil War anger still simmered and great numbers of uprooted men were adrift throughout the West, seeking a living whether honest or otherwise. "Otherwise" included not only things like the shady doings in Hidetown but also rustling, which increased steadily as trail herds brought higher and higher prices at the Kansas railroad towns. On the Clear Fork, as in other parts of Texas, the situation grew bad enough that some solid citizens turned lawless themselves and became vigilantes. A good many horse thieves and other malefactors ended up dangling from trees along the river, but rustlers kept taking their cut from ranchers' herds.

An interesting key figure in such events was an Alabamian named John M. Larn, a lethal young man evidently possessed of much charm when he chose to use it. He showed up at Griffin in about 1869 at the age of nineteen or twenty, having cowboyed in Colorado and New Mexico, where he is said to have killed a couple of men. On the Clear Fork he went to work for a rancher and was made foreman of a trail drive to Colorado, during which he killed two or three more people who somehow displeased him. Returning, he married a daughter of the respected Matthews ranching family, participated in the elimination of a band of suspected rustlers, joined the vigilantes, was sheriff at Griffin town for a short time, and acquired a ranch a few miles upstream from there on the old Camp Cooper reservation, where he built a fine stone house overlooking the river's broad valley.

In 1877 he and his close ally John Selman were appointed herd and hide inspectors by the county and also obtained a lucrative contract to furnish beef to the garrison of the fort. Shrinkage of Larn's neighbors' herds was soon noted, while his own maintained its numbers, and a citizens' posse with a warrant discovered hides weighted down in the Clear Fork below his house, bearing other people's brands. Other allegations surfaced, including one that Larn had murdered a couple of stonemasons and a carpenter to avoid paying them for their work. In reaction to growing hostility, he and Selman

with a few outlaw night riders began to terrorize the area, shooting at people's houses and killing stock. This drama finally ended in June of 1878, when he lay chained in a log jail at the county seat of Albany. There a midnight visit by masked and yellow-slickered vigilantes and a volley of .44-caliber lead put finish to the career of John M. Larn.

Selman was given a horse by some friends among the vigilantes, and was allowed to flee westward into a life whose ups and downs involved a good bit more outlawry. In later years he was a gambler and city constable in El Paso, where in 1895 he killed — assassinated, really — bad man John Wesley Hardin, and the following year was himself gunned down by a deputy U.S. marshal.

Concerning these men, Larn's own brother-in-law, rancher John A. "Bud" Matthews, observed, "John Selman was a dangerous man, but compared to John Larn, he was a gentleman. Larn was the meanest man I ever knew."

Near the handsome stone house that still gazes out across the Clear Fork valley, Larn's tall granite grave marker bears no epitaph, only his name and the dates that define his twenty-nine years of eventful existence on this planet.

Times moved along and got tamer. The cessation of Indian fighting had undermined Fort Griffin's reason for being. The wiping out of the buffalo herds — finished by 1878 — together with the end of the great trail drives and the arrival of the Texas Central railroad at Albany just to the south, did much the same thing to the Flat. The fort was abandoned in 1881 and its evocative ruins are now a Texas State Historical Site, on its hill above a plowed bottomland field where few traces remain of the town that once resounded with laughter, screams, curses, music, clinking glasses, hoofbeats, the rumble of hide wagons, and occasional gunfire.

Land-hungry ranchers and farmers continued to pour through toward the plains to the west, including the upper parts of the Clear Fork's basin, which had remained too dangerous for settlement before Palo Duro. Barbed wire showed up and, after some friction and resentful fence-cutting by landless individuals, soon did away with the open range. On their own enclosed territories, ranchers who had had the foresight to buy their land could now replace or upgrade the old longhorn strain with more productive English breeds. If so inclined, as some were, they could also stock their acreage more wisely, or for that matter could throw so many animals on it that it was soon bare ground except for brush and weeds. The region became mainly big-ranch country, with much farming where the terrain and the uncertain rainfall permitted. Spreads of forty or fifty thousand or more acres were common, as they still are today.

Some of these enterprises, including that of the Reynolds family and the SMS ranch founded by Swedish immigrant Svante Magnus Swenson, expanded into vast operations that controlled hundreds of thousands of acres in various parts of Texas and even in other states. A good many ranching clans, though, stayed put in the Clear Fork country, consolidating their holdings, building good lives, and producing some remarkably thoughtful and responsible children and grandchildren. Such people, it has seemed to me, are the main reason that Albany, Shackelford County's seat, is one of the most pleasant small towns in Texas. It lacks the dreary rows of deserted buildings common elsewhere, has much unjingoistic civic spirit and a first-rate art museum, and sponsors an annual, highly successful, outdoor musical pageant called the Fort Griffin Fandangle, in which practically the whole community participates on horseback, in buggies and wagons, or afoot.

If much credit for this distinctiveness must go to the old families — who for well over a century have been tradition-minded and keen on education, founding schools and sending their offspring off to good colleges — a share of the credit also has to go to oil and gas. Beginning in the Teens and Twenties of the century just past, these commodities were found and produced in all of the counties along the Clear Fork, with frantic booms in a few places and steady yields in others. The resulting augmentation of many ranchers' incomes enabled them not only to lead more thoughtful lives and send their offspring to college, but also to survive most of the varying evils that beset ranchers these days, not the least of which is an immense disparity between the market value of their land and the income its livestock produce. Petroleum engendered in the whole region a quiet prosperity that has lasted until today, with time out for the Great Depression and a couple of miserably extended drouths.

The Clear Fork's basin, like the river itself, has changed a good bit since virgin times. But where it has been decently cared for during the long era following the fencing of the range — mesquite and other invaders fought back from their eternal attempt to take over, pastures well-watered and not overgrazed — it is still strong cow country and as such very handsome, at least in the eyes of Texans who care about ranching and ranchers, as many of us, perhaps anachronistically, still do.

Maybe from the movies or Marlboro cigarette advertisements, many people seem to think of ranchers as surrounded by rugged country. Some of them are, of course, but the majority of cattle-raisers, from those on the early Asian steppes till now, have been plainsmen, because plains are where grass grows most abundantly. I never visit the Clear Fork region without recalling a spring day some years ago, when I was riding in a jeep with the late Watkins Reynolds Matthews, known to everyone as Watt, as he examined pastures and cattle on the ranch put together in the nineteenth century by his father.

Watt was probably in his mid-eighties at that point and had only stopped making such inspections from horseback a few years earlier, having been working at the ranch and later running it since his graduation from Princeton in 1921. He was a progressive man who took on new management practices when they made sense, while preserving many of the old ways, such as a permanent crew of capable hands.

His was one of those responsible families that had been on the Clear Fork since Indian times and were tied in tightly with its history. In fact, his mother, Sallie Reynolds Matthews, in her clear-minded seventies had set down quite a lot of that history in a charming and valuable series of early-day reminiscences. These were later put together in a book, entitled *Interwoven* because of the close relationships and many intermarriages of the Reynolds and Matthews families detailed in its pages, along with many old tales of frontier life.

At one point in the jeep ride we topped a low ridge and Watt stopped and turned off the engine. He waved a casual hand toward the valley that lay before us, two or three miles wide between our ridge and the one on its other side. It was thickly grassed, with scattered dark mottes of oaks, a couple of windmills, and only a sprinkling of stubborn mesquites with lacy new bright-green foliage. Here and there fat Herefords grazed. It was a classic and lovely scene, and I said so.

"Yes, it is," he said. "And you know the best thing about it?"

I shook my head.

He grinned and said, "There's not a single thing out there that would make a tourist stop and look twice."

He was not being hostile to outsiders. His remark, I believe, reflects the way that most real cattlemen have forever felt about their land. Fancy, rugged, Marlboro vistas are pleasant elsewhere, they know, but what counts most to them is country that's right for raising cows.

The Clear Fork has plenty of that.

SWINGING CORPSES, THE WORK OF VIGILANTE
GROUPS FROM THE "FLAT" AT FT. GRIFFITH,
WERE A COMMON SIGHT ALONG THIS STRETCH
OF RIVER IN THE MID-NINETEENTH CENTURY.

OPPOSITE: SPRING FLOWERS
BLANKET THE LANDSCAPE ALONG
THE RIVER IN MANY AREAS.

THE RIVER BENDS WESTWARD AT
THE OLD 1874 GRIST MILL SITE IN
THE RIVER TOWN OF ELIASVILLE.

EXCESSIVE UPRIVER WATER USE HAS LEFT
THE CONFLUENCE OF THE CLEAR FORK AND
SALT FORK DRY, EXCEPT IN WETTER TIMES.

NEXT SPREAD: THE SUTLER'S
STORE AT FORT GRIFFIN SERVED
SOLDIERS, BUFFALO HUNTERS AND
LONGHORN DROVERS, IN TURN.

OPPOSITE: NO LONGER IN USE,
THIS SUSPENSION BRIDGE
PROVIDED A ROUTE ACROSS THE
CLEAR FORK IN DAYS LONG PAST.

A RANCH ROAD CUTS A
MEANDERING PATH ALONG THE
RIVER AT REYNOLDS BEND.

NEXT SPREAD: WATT MATTHEWS AND
MANY OF HIS RELATIVES HAVE BEEN LAID
TO REST IN THE CEMETERY AT REYNOLDS
BEND, PART OF LAMBSHEAD RANCH.

THE HEADWATERS OF THE CLEAR FORK
BEGIN IN THE FEATURELESS
COTTON FIELDS NEAR ROTAN, TEXAS

FEW RIFFLES DISTURB THE
TRANQUIL CLEAR FORK ON ITS
JOURNEY THROUGH THE BIG
RANCH COUNTRY OF SHACKELFORD
AND THROCKMORTON COUNTIES.

The Spanish word for the

magnificent, tall, centuries-old

bald cypresses that line the banks of

the Sabinal is sabinos,

and sabinal means a grove of them.

The name still fits.

THE UPPER SABINAL

An Enclosed World

When white settlement of the Hill Country began, that region may have held other rivers as pretty as the little Sabinal in its upper reaches, but in our own time I have seen none to compare with it. It is one of the waterways that originate in springs of the rugged southern fringe of the limestone hills, west of San Antonio. A few miles downstream from sources in Real and Bandera counties, its two forks join to traverse a valley walled and dotted with low mountains, before the river finally and definitely leaves the hills behind, passing through a narrow groove in the Balcones Escarpment onto brushy plains, where porous soils absorb much of its flow and make it intermittent in many parts.

It is also one of the purest of our Texas rivers, possibly the purest of all, to judge by U.S. Geological Survey analyses of our streams. And, although the earliest white settlers arrived here a century and a half ago and started using the land hard, modern mankind seems to have exerted less pressure here on the

scheme of things than in most other regions. The upper river's drainage basin holds a rather sparse number of permanent residents, many of whom live in one quite small town, Utopia. It nurtures no pollutive industries, still depends heavily on ranching and on hunting leases, and has few of the kind of riverside vacation or retirement developments, fishing camps, and trailer parks so noticeable on other Hill Country streams.

Even more impressively, the magnificent, tall, centuries-old bald cypresses that line the banks of the Sabinal and some of its tributaries were spared from the nineteenth century's wholesale commercial exploitation of such trees for boards and shingles, which stripped so many of them from riversides elsewhere. What lumbering was done here was minor in scope and its products were put to local use. The Spanish word for these relatives of the redwood is *sabinos,* and *sabinal* means a grove of them. The name still fits.

Natives of this upper part of the

river refer to its basin, including the miles-wide valley, as the Canyon. The narrower slots that creeks have carved in the mountains on either side of both the main Sabinal and its West Prong are generally called hollows, rendered as "hollers" by local tongues. They form a network of fissures, steepest and most pronounced in the upper reaches of the West Prong in Real County, and in the Lost Maples area near the main river's sources.

There is more of the river, of course — the often intermittent stretch from the groove in the Escarpment to where the stream joins the Frio in southeastern Uvalde County. Along this flatter stretch there is one substantial town, called Sabinal, and in places where groundwater irrigation has been developed the land is sometimes lush these days. Most of it, though, is covered with a blanket of mesquite and thorny scrub that has been there just about forever — though I believe there is some scholarly disagreement over whether, long ago, it used to be a grassy savanna. This is the South Texas Brush Country, where a special kind of ranching and cowboying was evolved by Spaniards and Mexicans centuries ago and was passed along to Anglo interlopers. It is monotonous in appearance but has been much loved by its people, among them J. Frank Dobie, who was born and shaped in the same brush a few counties southeast of the Sabinal. In fact, Dobie used to come to this area often, to visit some kinfolks-by-marriage who ranched just north of the town of Sabinal, and to hunt deer and collect some of the folklore and treasure-hunting tales he wrote down in his books.

But let's get back to the Canyon.

Even among historians a certain amount of confusion seems to exist about the Indians who once frequented the Sabinal region. The tribes that were here originally — leaving out Paleo-Indians and Archaics, of whom there are many

traces — probably consisted of two or three wandering Coahuiltecan bands and some Tonkawas in the hills. But by the time San Antonio was established in 1718, or not long thereafter, Lipan Apaches had begun to predominate, shoved south and east out of their old Great Plains haunts by the Comanches' violent incursions. As time went on and Comanche depredations worsened, the Spanish tried to make the Apaches their allies by setting up presidios and missions for them, but this attempt failed. Most of the time the Apaches stayed at odds with both Comanches and Spaniards, and in 1790 Juan de Ugalde's troops won a battle with them in the Sabinal Canyon — which for a time was therefore called the Cañón de Ugalde. (The town and county of Uvalde were also named for this caballero, though the spelling got a bit corrupted along the way.)

Meanwhile the Comanches kept on coming, and coming. One of their main war and raiding trails passed from the Edwards Plateau down the Sabinal to the plains below and the Rio Grande, and they harried everybody they found along their route. This included the Anglo settlers who started arriving here in the early 1850s and were targets of hostility from both Comanches and Apaches, hostility which they returned full-strength. In the atmosphere of those times it is understandable that they didn't always know or care which tribe they were fighting at a given time and place, and old accounts often disagree about this. Things were further confused by the presence south of the Rio Grande of groups of displaced and disgruntled Indians, primarily Kickapoos but with some Apache cohorts, who in the resentful aftermath of the Mexican War were encouraged by Mexican authorities to raid up through South Texas, and did so with enthusiasm for many years.

It was a violent era with violent people on all sides, and there are plenty of old local tales deriving from it. Mrs. Kincheloe stuck full of arrows and lance wounds, but surviv-

ing. The exploits of Bigfoot Wallace, who ranched not far away and took part in many of the local pursuits of Indians. Frank Buckelew captured by Apaches as a kid and kept for several years, after which he remained quite Indianized, like old Herman Lehmann up in Mason County. The chase after eleven probably Comanche horse thieves that ended at a swimming hole on the Frio, the next river to the west, where the raiders, while happily splashing water, were all shot happily by their white pursuers, except for one who, happily or not, slipped away . . . And so on.

The Canyon's pioneers appear to have been an exceptionally sturdy and self-reliant lot. They needed to be. They were frontiersmen, but within the mountain-isolated environs they had chosen for their own, they were to some extent their own frontier, rather than part of a larger one as were settlers in regions with wider horizons. Supplies from outside were harder to come by, and so was help in coping with Indians — though for a time there was a Texas Ranger post at what is now the tiny hamlet of Vanderpool. So the settlers had to do their own coping for the most part.

The first of them was Captain William Ware, a veteran of San Jacinto who, with relatives and other followers and some livestock, came here in 1852, building his home on the river at a place below present Utopia that came to be known as Waresville. He died quite soon thereafter, though his descendants stayed on in the valley — the durable arrow-pierced Mrs. Kincheloe was one of his children. The year 1852 also saw the arrival of Gideon Thompson and his family, and others kept showing up in the years before the Civil War and afterward, acquiring land in patches large or small, building their dwellings with stone or cedar logs, and setting about making a living from their holdings.

Among these early settlers subsistence was the rule, raising things for home use — vegetables, corn and feed crops, and livestock both edible and usable for work — for there were no markets accessible from their isolated valley. Some, though, were more enterprising, like Gid Thompson, who was building a ranch operation in the upper Canyon with headquarters on the West Prong, where his stone house and fortress-like barn still stand. He saw the market potential in the swarms of Spanish longhorned cattle running wild in the valley and the Brush Country. They were free for the taking if you could handle them after you took them, and Thompson could. Even before the Civil War he assembled a herd and with his son Hiram and some cowboys drove them across the deserts to California, realizing a good profit from their sale. After the war he kept on doing this, and others began driving to California too, or to the railroad towns of Kansas when those trails opened up.

The war itself was a rough time around here, as it was everywhere else on the edge of Texas settlement. Federal garrisons withdrew from frontier posts, and though the only such post in this region, Fort Inge on the Leona near present Uvalde, was restaffed with state troops and Rangers, it was fifty miles or so from most settlers on the upper Sabinal and afforded scant protection from Comanches freed by the war for a widespread and bloody rampage. In addition, a number of local men had enlisted, though most joined state "home guard" units that operated in the region — which was not a hotbed of Rebel sentiment, Uvalde County having voted heavily against secession in the 1860 referendum.

At any rate, they coped, as they had coped before, "forting up" and fighting back, even though at times women and children had to be moved over to Fort Inge for protection. The ruling philosophy was perhaps best expressed by one old-timer: "To settle this part of Texas, all you had to do was fight the Comanches, the bears, and the wolves, survive the floods and outlast the drouths, and the land was yours." And after the war that attitude continued to prevail because it had to, though Indians stopped being a menace in the mid-1870s and the bears and wolves and panthers became mostly memories. By then the area's population was taking on an admixture of hardy German-speaking Alsatians moving west out of the Castro colonies in Medina County, who shaped up their own farms and ranches and often intermarried with the Anglo families.

The Canyon was never a prosperous place, and self-sufficiency remained the norm even after some sources of cash were developed besides trail-driven longhorns. Cotton became a crop on the good soils of the valley floor, and was produced in quantity until a massive invasion of boll weevils in the Nineties wiped out that activity. Sheep and especially Angora goats thrived on the brushy slopes of the mountains, yielding wool and mohair salable for cash when hauled in wagons up onto the Divide above Lost Maples, then down the Guadalupe to Kerrville, or sometimes westward to Rocksprings. The advent of barbed wire stimulated the breeding of meatier cattle with British blood, and after the railroad reached Sabinal in 1881, trail drives became quite short.

But no irrelevant booms like those created by oil and other mineral discoveries ever visited the Sabinal, nor did its climate change. Too much rain and too little have been the lasting threats. I have read that the precipitous country along the Balcones Fault is more subject to flash flooding than anywhere else in this nation, and floods have struck here a number of times, destroying homesteads and fences and fields and drowning livestock and people. Utopia, first named Montana, was established in the 1880s primarily because Waresville, just to its south, had been so often inundated.

Less quickly devastating, drouths crept in unannounced and created a deadly stasis in which nothing grew and even the river might stop running, except underground and in one or two deep holes. People tried to keep coping, and often did, by preserving food in good years against the possibility of bad ones, but sometimes that wasn't enough, as during the drouths of the late Teens and the Thirties, when some natives took up moonshining or other fringe activities to survive, while many others left to seek jobs elsewhere, the canneries and fruit orchards of California being favored destinations. Another large exodus took place during the horrendous dry years of the Fifties, at the end of which Utopia is reported to have held only sixty persons.

Today the Canyon is of course much changed from its original state, if less than a lot of other Texas land. Brush Country vegetation has spread into places where once, as an oldster put it, "The grass was horse high and not a mesquite in sight." Cedars proliferating on overgrazed slopes suck away a fat share of the valley's water, shrinking the creeks and the river. And the range of wildlife species has been greatly impoverished. All of which ills, in one form or another, are common throughout our state and our country — the price, as my hydrologist friend in Washington observed, that we have paid for modern times.

The dozens of working ranches occupying that altered landscape range in size from modest to eight or ten thousand acres. A few belong to absentee city owners, but surprisingly many are still in the hands of descendants of the old-timers. Nearly all are more carefully managed than they used to be, because of hard-earned awareness of what kind of use will restore the land to some extent and guard it against further decline.

In human terms, a large change has been the virtual disappearance of a number of small rural neighborhoods that used to be sprinkled about the Canyon, centered on small schools and on family relationships. Their names are remem-

bered and even used — the Harper Settlement, the Taylor Community, Valley View, Little Creek, and others — but modern communications and transport have done away with their reason for existence and their intimate sense of locale.

Still another difference from the old days, small but very visible, dates back mainly, I believe, to the 1950s — the construction of concrete channel dams here and there on the river. These create pleasant long blue pools that more or less duplicate the natural "holes" much cherished by the old ones for swimming, fishing, revivals, and baptizings. But they can be hard on shoreline cypresses, especially it seems the larger ones, which often don't tolerate the change in water level, and die. "Cypresses," one local said to me with conviction, "don't much like change."

The Canyon possesses tourist attractions, chief among them its overall scenic beauty, epitomized in the Texas Parks and Wildlife Department's Lost Maples State Natural Area that straddles the river's main fork high up in jagged, handsome country. There are some bed-and-breakfasts, a couple of them quite upscale, and one small motel. Utopia puts on an annual rodeo, with barbecues, that is much attended by outsiders. And plenty of lease-hunters show up in autumn to harvest the area's numerous if rather small deer, of which around 900 are processed each year at a Utopia facility. There is even to be a sesquicentennial celebration in 2002. . . .

Yet none of this seems to have done much to diminish the place's essential peace and calm, which leads an observer to wonder why not. Why has its attractiveness not spawned the sort of frantic real-estate development and the construction of hotels, motels, and gaudy fun centers that blight so much of the rest of our Hill Country nowadays? Why do the river's stately cypress corridors, where often the only sounds

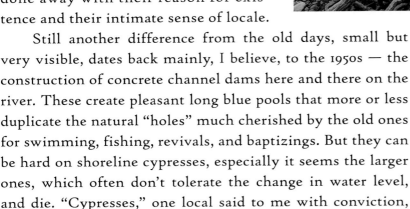

are the rippling of water and the songs of birds, lack windrows of empty beer cans and loud flotillas of innertubers?

Another, related question delves back much farther: Why are the cypresses still here? How did the Sabinal manage to escape the effects of our forebears' addiction to their lumber ("the wood eternal," it was called), which demolished so many of those superb trees throughout the region?

What is it, in short, that makes this enclave so distinctively non-twenty-first-century?

I put these questions to a knowledgeable, educated younger local man, descended from one of the place's old families and related to some of the other ones. He lives in a city now, but feels his home territory's pull, visits it often, and plans to bring his family there to live when he can do so.

He smiled and said the one about cypresses was the easiest to answer. Huge logs or even big loads of lumber couldn't be hauled out of the Canyon by oxen on the narrow, winding, rough, steep trails that used to be the only exits. "Mr. John Leakey lived here for a while in the 1850s, but then he moved over on the Frio where the town is named for him. He built his sawmill there, and you can still see some of the stumps."

As for the people's resistance to outside ways, he thought that might have derived from the same isolation, which was often hard on the early folk but also contributed to a sense of specialness and to the self-reliance we have noted, which got passed down. "Our people have been through too many hard times to be called self-satisfied," he said, "though there may be a touch of that."

This makes sense to an alien like myself. Nearly all of the true natives I have met on the Sabinal have been friendly and generous-spirited people, but there is a part of them that is hard for an outsider to reach. I think it has to do with their strong attachment to place, which used to be common among rural Americans but is less and less so now, and with an awareness

that outsiders, however sympathetic, are still outsiders, even if a number of quiet retirees and others who fit in do find acceptance. The natives' traditions, family memories, and ingrained awareness of their countryside's past constitute a mythology which, in W. B. Yeats's phrase, "marries them to rock and hill." They cherish their Canyon as an extension of themselves and their ancestors, and, in the manner of the cypresses, they "don't much like change."

Or is that wishful thinking, and do plenty of natives actually yearn for wholesale, garish, and cash-generating change in their river and their surroundings? Looking at other valleys not far away, one has to consider that possibility.

The area's young people, raised with television and computers and much aware of a wider world, also pose a question. Will they be as protective of what is here as their elders have been, as aware of its mythology? The friend who answered my other questions says that after he graduated from Utopia High School, he couldn't wait to get away, and he adds that most local youths still feel that way, and leave. But in time, with the perspective that absence bestows, he began to see the valley's unique qualities and came to cherish his connection with it. And he believes that many others who leave gain similar insight and will want to return later on: "We leave as soon as we can, and then spend the rest of our lives trying to figure out how to get back."

At any rate, for now — despite the dents and scars of history, and whatever the reasons and prospects may be — the Sabinal Canyon is still blessedly, tranquilly, and beautifully itself.

A lot of us, whether natives or strangers, devoutly hope it may remain so.

Will it?

WILD IVY FLOURISHES
ALONG THE LUSH
BANKS OF THE SABINAL.

OPPOSITE: REFERRED TO BY LOCALS AS
"THE BLUE WATER HOLE," THIS DEEP
FRAGMENT OF THE SABINAL HAS OFFERED
AN OASIS DURING PERIODS OF DROUTH.

PREVIOUS SPREAD: THE FRIO-
SABINAL DIVIDE PRESENTED A
SIGNIFICANT OBSTACLE TO EARLY
SETTLERS TRAVELING BY WAGON.

HIGH IN THE SABINAL VALLEY THE
WEST PRONG OF THE RIVER SNAKES ITS
PATH SOUTHWARD TO JOIN THE MAIN
CHANNEL ABOVE THE TOWN OF UTOPIA.

OCCASIONAL PERIODS OF HEAVY RAIN OVERLOAD
THE SHALLOW SOILS OF THE SABINAL VALLEY,
TRANSFORMING THE NORMALLY PLACID STREAM
INTO A TURBID AND DANGEROUS TORRENT.

OPPOSITE: THE TRANQUILLITY OF
THE SABINAL VALLEY ATTRACTS
VISITORS FROM ACROSS THE STATE.

THE ECONOMIC BASES OF THE SABINAL
VALLEY ARE NATIVE AND EXOTIC
WILDLIFE, CATTLE, GOATS, AND SHEEP.

NEXT SPREAD: THE RIVER
DERIVES MOST OF ITS FLOW
FROM SPRINGS ISSUING FROM
THE CANYONLANDS ABOVE.

FROSTY AUTUMN AIR AND WARMER
WATER COMBINE TO PRODUCE A
LIGHT FOG THAT DIFFUSES THE
RAYS OF SUNRISE OVER THE RIVER.

CYPRESS ROOTS SIPHON IMMENSE
QUANTITIES OF WATER TO SUPPORT
THE MASSIVE TREES GROWING
ALONG THE RIVER'S BANKS.

THE UPPER SABINAL
VALLEY'S LOST
MAPLES STATE PARK
LURES THOUSANDS OF
VISITORS ANNUALLY.

OPPOSITE: TOO MUCH RAIN, AS WELL AS TOO
LITTLE, HAVE PRESENTED CHALLENGES TO THOSE
WHO MAKE THE SABINAL REGION THEIR HOME.

BIBLIOGRAPHY

In the completion of this endeavor many publications were helpful, of which some undoubtedly got left out of the following list. Editions noted are the ones used, regardless of earlier or later issues of the works.

GENERAL

Fehrenbach, T. R., *Comanches: the Destruction of a People.* New York, Alfred A. Knopf, 1974.

Holden, William Curry, *Alkali Trails, or Social and Economic Movements of the Texas Frontier, 1846–1900.* Lubbock, Texas Tech University Press, 1998.

Huser, Verne, *Rivers of Texas.* College Station, Texas A&M Press, 2000.

Kingston, Mike, editor, *Texas Almanac, 1994–95.* Dallas, *The Dallas Morning News,* 1995.

Newcomb, W. W., Jr., *The Indians of Texas.* Austin, University of Texas Press, 1961.

Priddy, B. L. "Bud," *Fly-fishing the Texas Hill Country.* Austin, W. Thomas Taylor, 1994.

Texas Parks and Wildlife Department, *An Analysis of Texas Waterways.* College Station, Texas Agricultural Extension Service, 1974.

Tyler, Ron, editor-in-chief, *The New Handbook of Texas.* Six volumes. Austin, Texas State Historical Association, 1996.

United States Geological Survey topographic maps, 1/24,000 and 1/100,000, covering all of the watersheds in this book.

Wallace, Ernest, and E. Adamson Hoebel, *The Comanches, Lords of the South Plains.* Norman, University of Oklahoma Press, 1952.

THE CANADIAN

Erickson, John, *Through Time and the Valley.* Austin, Shoal Creek Publishers, 1978.

Haley, J. Evetts, *The XIT Ranch of Texas.* Norman, University of Oklahoma Press, 1967.

Rathjen, Frederick W., *The Texas Panhandle Frontier,* revised edition. Lubbock, Texas Tech University Press, 1998.

THE LOWER NECHES

Abernethy, Francis, editor, *Tales from the Big Thicket.* Austin, University of Texas Press, 1966

Ely, Glen Sample, producer, *The Big Thicket of Southeast Texas: A History, 1800–1940* (videotape). Austin, Forest Glen TV Productions, 1988.

Peacock, Howard, *Nature Lover's Guide to the Big Thicket.* College Station, Texas A&M University Press, 1994.

Sitton, Thad, *Backwoodsmen: Stockmen and Hunters along a Big Thicket River Valley.* Norman, University of Oklahoma Press, 1995.

Truett, Joe C., and Daniel W. Lay, *Land of Bears and Honey, a Natural History of East Texas.* Austin, University of Texas Press, 1984.

Wright, Solomon A., *My Rambles as East Texas Cowboy, Hunter, Fisherman, Tie-cutter,* as quoted in Truett and Lay, above. Austin, Texas Folklore Society, 1942.

THE PECOS

Dearen, Patrick, *Crossing Rio Pecos.* Fort Worth, Texas Christian University Press, 1996.

_____, *A Cowboy of the Pecos.* Plano, Republic of Texas Press, 1997.

Ely, Glen Sample, producer, *Graveyard of the West: the Pecos River of Texas, where Myth Meets History* (videotape). Austin, Forest Glen TV Productions, 1993.

Haley, J. Evetts, *Charles Goodnight, Cowman and Plainsman.* Norman, University of Oklahoma Press, 1949.

Newcomb, W.W., Jr. (text), and Forrest Kirkland (paintings), *The Rock Art of Texas Indians.* Austin, University of Texas Press, 1967.

Skiles, Jack, *Judge Roy Bean Country.* Lubbock, Texas Tech University Press, 1996.

THE BRAZOS CLEAR FORK

Clayton, Lawrence, and Joan Halford Farmer, editors, *Tracks Along the Clear Fork: Stories from Shackelford and Throckmorton Counties.* Abilene, McWhiney Foundation Press, 2000.

Greene, A. C., *A Personal Country.* New York, Alfred A. Knopf, 1969.

Holden, Frances Mayhugh, *Lambshead After Interwoven, a Texas Range Chronicle, 1848–1878.* College Station, Texas A&M University Press, 1982.

Ledbetter, Barbara, *Fort Belknap: Frontier Saga.* Burnet, Eakin Press, 1982.

Matthews, Sallie Reynolds, *Interwoven, a Pioneer Chronicle.* College Station, Texas A&M University Press, 1982.

Newcomb, Samuel P., unpublished diary of life at Fort Davis, Stephens County, in 1865.

THE LLANO

Biesele, Rudolph L., *The History of the German Settlements in Texas, 1831–1861.* German-Texan Historical Society, San Marcos, Texas, 1987.

Greene, A.C., *The Last Captive.* Austin, The Encino Press, 1972. (Herman Lehmann's story as reconstructed and annotated by Greene.)

Hadeler, Glenn, "The Mason County Hoodoo Wars" (Part I) and "Terror in the Hills, the Mason County 'Hoodoo' War" (Part II). *Enchanted Rock Magazine,* 1998.

Jordan, Gilbert J., *Yesterday in the Texas Hill Country.* College Station, Texas A&M University Press, 1979.

Jordan, Terry, *German Seed in Texas Soil.* Austin, University of Texas Press, 1994.

THE UPPER SABINAL

Bush, Peter W., et al: *Water Quality in South-Central Texas, 1996-98.* USGS Circular 1212, 2000.

Walton, Greg, collector & editor, *Bear Meat'n' Honey, an Oral History of the Sabinal Canyon, Volume I.* Austin, Acorn Press, 1990.

_____, *Coyote Songs, an Oral History of the Sabinal Canyon, Volume II.* Austin, Acorn Press, 1999.

Publisher Susan L. Ebert
Project Manager Larry D. Hodge
Managing Editor Mary-Love Bigony
Production Editor Regina Fuentes

Texas Rivers was designed by Nancy McMillen
Nancy McMillen Design, Austin

Text and display type are set in Hightower Text Roman
and Hightower Text Italic from The Font Bureau, Inc.

This book is printed on Saber 70# Gloss Book
Dust jacket is printed on Lustro 100# Gloss Book
End sheets are 75# text weight Classic Laid, Camel Hair
Case is wrapped in ICG Holliston, by Arrestox

Scanning and color by Daniel Gipp,
electronic pre-press by Vertis, Inc., San Antonio

Electronic prep and printing by Best Press, Inc., Addison, Texas

*Special thanks to Brazos Mutual Fund for their
generous support in helping this book be published and in funding
a state-wide traveling exhibit based on the book.*